History of Finland

A Captivating Guide to Finnish History

Free Bonus from Captivating History
(Available for a Limited time)

Hi History Lovers!

Now you have a chance to join our exclusive history list so you can get your first history ebook for free as well as discounts and a potential to get more history books for free! Simply visit the link below to join.

Captivatinghistory.com/ebook

Also, make sure to follow us on Facebook, Twitter and Youtube by searching for Captivating History.

Table of Contents

Introduction

Finland (called *Suomi* in Finnish) was in the news a lot in 2022. It has long been a non-aligned country that walked a tightrope between Russia to its east and the NATO countries to the west. Two words that describe the Finns of the 20th and 21st centuries are "fiercely independent." Still, they can only maintain that independence by standing alone in a Europe that has long been divided between East and West.

Why are the Finns so fiercely independent? Well, until 1917, Finland was ruled by outsiders—the Swedes to the west and Russians to the east—for centuries. From the times of the Vikings, areas of Finland (and sometimes even the whole country) were not "Finnish." Imagine if the British had ruled the United States from the 1600s to today. The Finns' lives would have been similar. They were subjects of outside kings, queens, and tsars until just over one hundred years ago.

Finland became formally independent in 1918 after Vladimir Lenin, the leader of the Soviet Union, officially recognized the "new" country on January 4th, 1918.

Until 2022, that independence was contingent, to one degree or another, on Finland maintaining a balance in its relationship with the Soviet Union/Russia and the West. Officially "non-aligned" with either side, Finland found itself in a position of influence with the two sides. The Finns had good relationships with both sides and often hosted or sponsored talks between them.

Still, while Finland is a relatively large country in Europe, it was dwarfed by the USSR and unfortunately found itself at odds with it in 1939 when Soviet ruler Joseph Stalin decided to reclaim Finland and annex it into the USSR as a socialist republic. Suffice it to say that while Stalin did not achieve all of his goals, the war did not go well for Finland, though it retained its independence through the brave resistance of its outnumbered soldiers.

After WWII, with Stalin at Finland's doorstep, the Finns renewed their neutrality pledge. Though constantly under the watchful eye of the Soviets, the situation benefited the Finns to a significant degree. They were one of the few Western countries with open doors to Soviet business, and a huge amount of trade in machinery, telecommunications, and much else flowed into the USSR from Finland. The Finns also did business with the countries of western and central Europe, most of whom were NATO (North Atlantic Treaty Organization) members.

The fall of the Soviet Union in 1991 and the formation of the Russian Federation did not change Russia's relationship with Finland. But when Vladimir Putin took power in Russia and gradually began asserting Russian nationalism and boasting of a massive military buildup, Finland's relationship with Russia began to change.

Though still officially non-aligned (a policy approved by most Finns until quite recently), the country began to shift slowly toward NATO. Russian submarine patrols in Finnish waters and occasional overflights of its border regions pushed the Finns, like it did the similarly non-aligned Swedes, toward the United States and western Europe. In the ten or so years before the invasion of Ukraine in 2022, Finnish forces took part in military exercises with NATO, and its intelligence services began to work more closely with the West.

Finland shares an eight-hundred-mile border with Russia. When Putin invaded Ukraine, which had once been a part of the Soviet Union, Finland wisely decided that it might be next in Putin's plans to restore Russian "glory." In spring 2022, the Finns and the Swedes applied for NATO membership, which is being fast-tracked as of this writing.

A new era has begun for Finland.

A Few Facts and Figures About Finland

Finland is one of the Nordic countries. Looking carefully, you'll see that the word's meaning is easily deduced. In most Germanic languages (Finnish is not one of them), *Nord* means "north." Many people mistakenly lump Finland in with its western neighbors of Norway, Sweden, and Denmark, the Scandinavian countries.

Scandinavia has its roots in both Latin and Old German. The Romans called the region *Scandinovia* for a new and prosperous island, which, of course, was wrong. They likely got the name from the Old German word *Scadinavia*. In Old Norse, Skaney means "south end of Sweden." In the older Proto-German language, the words are *Skaðin* and *Awjō*, meaning "dangerous island" or "dangerous land next to water," likely referring to the rugged coastline of Norway and the frequent bad weather in the region.

Scandinavians speak languages from the German language tree. The Finns, along with the Hungarians and Estonians, speak a language from the Finno-Uralic tree, which originated in northern Russia and the Ural Mountains.

Of the 193 countries in the United Nations, Finland is sixty-sixth in size. Over 10 percent of its 338,145 square kilometers consists of lakes. Much of the rest of the nation, especially away from its capital of Helsinki, is forested, and the Finns have been quite careful to keep it that way. Generally speaking, Finns pride themselves on being "outdoor people," even if they don't camp and "rough it" all the time.

The population of Finland is quite small for its size. In 2022, it had 5.6 million people. Though the country is 66th in size, it is 116th in population. There are 16.36 people per square mile. Finland is about 83 percent the size of California. California had a population of 37 million and a population density of 251.3 people per square mile in 2019.

Finland is not crowded, and its people like it that way. A popular joke in Finland during the recent pandemic had to do with social distancing. Since Finland is sparsely populated and the Finns are perceived as being people who like their space and privacy, T-shirts and signs mocking the need for social distancing popped up all over. It wasn't that the Finns believed the disease was a hoax (on the contrary, they were quite prepared for it). No, it was just that social distancing was already a thing in Finland. One T-shirt had a Finnish flag with the words "Social Distancing" below it. Under that was this phrase, "I'm Finnish. I've been preparing for this my whole life."

As you discovered earlier, Finland is bordered by Russia. It also shares a long border with Sweden and a smaller border with Norway above the Arctic Circle. Speaking of the Arctic Circle, Finland is cold in fall and winter, though most of the country lies beneath the Arctic Circle. Still, on average, Finland is relatively temperate, at least for its location. The Baltic and North Atlantic currents bring warmer water and air to the coasts, and the lakes have a great effect on the weather as well.

In June 2022, the average temperatures in Helsinki in the south and the city of Sodankylä in the north were 15.9°C/60.6°F and 13.8°C/56.8°F, respectively. In January 2020, a generally warmer year worldwide, Helsinki's average temperature was -3.4°C/25.8°F and -9.5°C/14.9°F in Sodankylä. Despite the warming trends of the waters, Finland is cold, and for much of the year, there is not much sun. Its lack of sunlight has to do with its location in the far north, which sees longer nights in the winter, but the weather also plays a role. Surrounded by water on three sides, there are far more cloudy days than sunny days in Finland. Sunny days in Finland generally see crowds of people outside soaking up all the sunshine they can get.

Finland is not mountainous. Most of its territory is flat, especially in the south, but there are large numbers of rolling hills and plains. A little over 70 percent of Finland is forest, and only 7.5 percent is arable (suitable for farming). Finland was once a nation with large numbers of farmers, including dairy farmers, but even when much of the population worked in agriculture, the Finns had to import most of its food. Finland faced hunger and, at times, starvation throughout its history.

Natural Resources

Finland contains and produces a variety of natural resources. As you might assume from a country covered by trees, its primary resource is timber. Like Norway and Sweden, its neighbors to the west, Finland also contains significant deposits of lead, nickel, gold, silver, limestone, copper, and iron ore. It also has a large fishing industry.

Population and Ethnic Groups

Finland's population in 2022 was 5,601,547. New York City alone has more people than Finland. The country is sparsely populated and likely has been throughout its history.

Finns, Swedes, Estonians, Romani, Russians, and the native Sami are the largest ethnic groups. The intertwined history of Finland and Sweden means that it is likely that many Finns have Swedish ancestors. The Romani people have enjoyed, for the most part, living in Finland compared to other countries, as Finland has been traditionally less discriminatory toward them than European countries in the south.

Language

Finland has two official languages: Finnish and Swedish. For centuries, Finland was a Swedish territory, and much of the western part of Finland was populated by Swedes. The Swedes and much of the urban and upper-class population of Finland spoke only Swedish. This very slowly began to change after Finland was given to Russia in an 1809 treaty, but even into the 20th century, many of the ruling and educated classes spoke Swedish.

In a 2008 poll, Finns voted Carl Gustav Emil Mannerheim (most often known as just Mannerheim), the leader of Finland for much of the first half of the 20th century, as the "greatest Finn of all time." Mannerheim had Swedish and German roots and struggled to speak Finnish. It is estimated that only about 6 percent of Finns spoke Swedish at home in 2022.

Other languages include Estonian, Russian, Romani, and three Sami languages: Inari Sami, Skolt Sami, and Northern Sami. The majority of Finns speak English to some degree or another. Most speak English fairly well and even fluently.

Finnish, like Estonian and its distant cousin Hungarian, is quite difficult to learn. Strangely enough, these three languages are more related to the Turkic languages of Central Asia and Turkey than they are to any of the Scandinavian and European languages.

Even if you cannot speak Finnish, you can easily recognize it in print. Finnish uses a lot of vowels and has many different vowel sounds. The letter "e" is the most commonly used letter in English, but "e" is not used as frequently in Finnish as "o," "u," and "a."

Finnish also contains many examples of double consonants, particularly "l" and "k."

English: "Finland is a beautiful country with a lot of trees and lakes."

Swedish: "Finland är ett vackert land med många träd och sjöar."

Finnish: "Suomi on kaunis maa, jossa on paljon puita ja järviä."

Estonian: "Soome on ilus maa, kus on palju puid ja järvi."

Hungarian: "Finnország egy gyönyörű ország, sok fával és tavakkal."

Religion

Most Finns describe themselves as Lutheran. However, as in most Western countries, church attendance in Finland has declined over the last few decades. Fully a third of Finns say they are not religious at all. There is a small percentage of Finns who are Eastern Orthodox who live mostly near the Russian border. Russia is a predominantly Orthodox country, so this makes sense. Another small percent of the population is Muslim; they are mostly immigrants or descendants of immigrants from the Middle East. Most Muslims live in larger cities, such as Helsinki and Turku.

The national flag of Finland.
https://commons.wikimedia.org/wiki/File:Flag_of_Finland.svg

Government

We will be discussing the evolution of Finland from a Swedish and Russian territory ruled by various forms of a monarchy to the representative democratic government it is today. But for the moment, it is enough to know that the Finns have a unicameral legislature (one chamber as opposed to two like in the United States).

The president is the chief of state and largely conducts foreign affairs internationally but with the input and influence of the government through the prime minister and the legislature. The prime minister is elected by the people and runs the government. They are responsible for creating laws and policies that are then voted on by the legislature (the Eduskunta). The president is elected once every six years, providing stability. The prime minister is more dependent on political support within the Eduskunta, and the position is sometimes more tenuous than that of the president, depending on party politics and popularity.

As of this writing (fall 2022), Finland's president is Sauli Niinistö. He has served since 2012. The president has a two-term limit and serves for six years per term. The prime minister is Sanna Marin, who became the youngest world leader in 2019 at the age of thirty-four and the youngest prime minister in the country's history. Marin has been somewhat controversial in Finland, not so much because of her policies but because of her age, gender, and appearance, all of which have provoked deep discussions and arguments within Finland over the role and behavior of women in society.

Chapter 1 – Prehistory

It was not until the advent of Christianity in Scandinavia that we really learned much about the people of Finland. Archaeologists are learning more all the time, but compared to other nations, especially other European nations, our knowledge of Finland and the people who lived there is relatively scant.

In 1996, a number of interesting stone objects were found in Wolf Cave on the coast of central western Finland. From 1997 to 2000, paleontologists, archaeologists, and other scientists worked in the cave to determine the origin of these objects, which included two hundred artifacts and about six hundred pieces of what is believed to be "strike waste," the chips from when stone is pounded or pressed against another stone to make sharp stone tools. Some of the artifacts were made of minerals that do not naturally occur in the area, causing speculation that they were brought from outside, possibly by Neanderthals, some 120,000 to 130,000 years ago.

There were also large amounts of animal bones and skeletons of various sizes. In two deeper layers of soil, there seemed to be evidence of signs that the ground had been packed down by humans, animals, or both, though the animal bones themselves were found in the top layer of the soil, with the bones dating to only about eight thousand years ago.

Wolf Cave shortly after its discovery.
https://commons.wikimedia.org/wiki/File:Varggrottan_1998..jpg

Work is still ongoing in Wolf Cave, though it is slow since the site is dangerous with the constant threat of cave-ins. Prehistorians in Finland and elsewhere are still debating on the origin of the bones and stone, with some insisting that they are evidence of Neanderthal settlement, at least for a time, in Wolf Cave. If this is true, it would be the only evidence of Neanderthals in any of the Nordic countries. While that does not mean that the people who lived in Wolf Cave were not Neanderthals, it makes the chances of it a bit less likely.

Other scientists believe that the cave was underwater for the time period in question, while others do not. It's also possible that the implements found in the cave come from a much later time period. Studies continue, but as of this writing, the people who live near Wolf Cave in the town of Karijoki derive some income from a small tourist trade.

What We Do Know About Ancient Finland

We know that parts of Finland were occupied by at least 8500 BCE during the Stone Age. Actually, the period is best known as the last glacial period or the last ice age. These people were hunter-gatherers who likely traveled throughout the area, perhaps including southern Sweden and northern Russia.

About three thousand years later, knowledge and culture from other parts of Europe began to arrive in Finland. In mainland Europe, the Corded Ware culture was present. It was one of a series of cultures that replaced or built on those that had come before. In Finland, the Corded Ware culture is the first known culture to have created more advanced tools from the molding and firing of clay. The name "Corded Ware" comes from the culture's pottery (in the form of urns, pots, and smaller containers), which has a purposefully artistic corded design.

The Corded Ware culture existed not only in Finland but also in a large arc from central Europe to Scandinavia to the plains of central Russia from circa 3000 to 2350 BCE. Toward the end of the period, it is possible that semi-permanent, semi-agricultural settlements were built, at least in the southern part of Finland or near the coasts where the weather was a bit warmer. However, the development of Finnish agriculture was slow compared to other parts of Europe due to the lingering effects of the cold climate brought about by the last glacial period.

Typical Nordic decorative stone axes.

The later Finnish Corded Ware culture differed from those in other parts of Europe to a degree and has its own name: Finnish Battle Ax culture. It was named after the soapstone and decorative stone axes found throughout much of Finland. Since the discovery of these battle axes, debate has raged between Swedish and Finnish archaeologists about whether these cultures were the same people and whether a particular territory was the "home" of the culture or not.

The next significant change in Finland was the arrival of the Bronze Age, which is generally considered to have lasted from about 3300 to 1200 BCE, though the Bronze Age in Finland began and ended later than it did in more temperate and centrally located parts of Europe and Eurasia.

It's believed that bronze technology came to Finland from the area of the Altai Mountains, where China, Russia, Mongolia, and Kazakhstan meet. The earliest bronze implements found in Finland greatly resemble other artifacts from what is called the Seima-Turbino phenomenon, named for the places where these types of artifacts were first found. The term "phenomenon" is used because this tool-making culture spread in almost all directions for a relatively short period of time, just two hundred years, between 2100 and 1900 BCE.

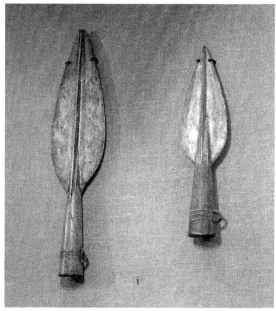

Seima-Turbino spearheads found at Borodino, Russia
Лапоть, CC0, via Wikimedia Commons https://en.wikipedia.org/wiki/Seima-Turbino_phenomenon#/media/File:Spearheads_1_Seima-Turbino_GIM.jpg

Artifacts from the Seima-Turbino phenomenon have been found in Korea, Japan, northeast China, the Russian Far East, Finland, and parts of Sweden. It's also possible that the Uralic roots of the Finnish language come from the time of this phenomenon.

The Bronze Age ushered in greater Finnish contact with the outside world. Previously, what trade existed between the people in Finland and other places occurred with those who inhabited modern-day Estonia, just across the Gulf of Finland. There may also have been trade routes overland from the southern Finnish area through the area around modern St. Petersburg to Estonia.

People in Finland began to make their own style of bronze tools and weapons around 1300 BCE and also began to import quantities of bronze from the Volga region of Russia, southern Sweden, and Norway. Though Finland remained a mystery to many people outside the region for quite some time, there was contact between people in the region, even if it was only on the coasts.

The Iron Age and the Roman Age

The Bronze Age in Finland lasted longer than it did in other parts of Europe, ending only in about 500 BCE with the coming of the Iron Age. Artifacts dated from 500 to 1 BCE indicate no real signs of contact with the great civilizations of the Mediterranean, the Middle East, or Asia. This time is called the Pre-Roman Period.

The Roman Period of the Finnish Iron Age began in 1 CE and ended around 400 CE (roughly about the time of the fall of the Western Roman Empire). As you may know, if you have read about other Nordic cultures of the time, the people of modern Norway, Sweden, and Denmark were what some historians call pre-literate, meaning they had a runic (and rudimentary) alphabet and did not keep written records of any great length or meaning beyond runestones and inscriptions on bones. Their written records indicated possession or perhaps a short snippet about boundary lines or the death of a kinsman or friend. The people of Finland may have had a runic alphabet, like the Estonians of the time. However, no written documents or artifacts from Finland from the period are known to exist.

The first written reference to the people of Finland comes from the Roman historian Tacitus in his book, *On the Origin and Situation of the Germans*, which is usually referred to as the *Germania*. Tacitus's work encompasses the lands of modern Germany and parts of Austria, Poland, Denmark, Sweden, Norway, and Finland.

Tacitus's book describes in great (but not always accurate or subjective) detail the Germanic people of present-day mainland Europe and ends with brief references to the people of Estonia, whom he called the Æsti and the Fenni. In his book, Tacitus admits that he does not know how to classify the Fenni, as he is unsure if they were German people or Sarmatians, people who lived in parts of

Ukraine and Central Asia near the Caspian Sea and Persia. Even in Roman times, people were confused about which group the Finns belonged to, much in the same way that people today sometimes call the Finns "Scandinavians."

Tacitus never traveled to Finland or most of the other places he wrote about. He relied on word of mouth and ancient writings, although he probably sprinkled in some imagination as well. But even though the following quote does not paint the Fenni in a great light, Tacitus does indicate a bit of respect for them at the end of his book:

"The Fenni are astonishingly savage and disgustingly poor. They have no proper weapons, no horses, no homes. They eat wild herbs, dress in skins, and sleep on the ground ... Yet they count their lot happier than that of others who groan over field labor, sweat over house-building, or hazard their own and other men's fortunes in the hope of profit and the fear of loss. Unafraid of anything that man or god can do to them, they have reached a state that few human beings can attain: for these men are so well content that they do not even need to pray for anything."

Some other Roman writings describe the area that was occupied by the Finns. There are also place names that indicate permanent settlements on the coast. Additionally, there are also the names of a number of ancient Finnish kings and a few descriptions of their culture. However, Finland remains a mystery for the most part until well into the Early Middle Ages.

The Finns are mentioned a couple of times in the annals of the Frankish Empire during the time of Charlemagne, but the annals only mention the Finnish name for the country, *Suomi*, and a man who signed some type of peace agreement.

Two runestones in Sweden mention Finland as *finlont* and *finlandi*, but that is all the mentions of Finland until the writer of many famous Scandinavian sagas, Snorri Sturluson, talks about the land and people of Finland in *Egil's Saga*. Snorri tells of a war in the far northeast of Finland between a mixed Norwegian/Finnish war band and the Karelian people, who live in the territory between Archangel and St. Petersburg, Russia, today.

In the 12th and 13th centuries, the mentions of Finland and the Finns begin to increase. This happened due to increased Swedish activity in the country, mostly in the form of missionaries and Swedish rulers' interest in forced Christianization.

Contact with the Outside World Grows: 400–800 CE

Though there is not one moment that marks the "end" of the Roman Empire, at least in western Europe, it was in decline for over one hundred years when the Migration Period began around 400 CE.

The empire had been the glue that held the many people of western and southern Europe together. With the end of the empire and of the Roman army as a dominating force, many people in Europe began to move. At the same time, people from the steppes of modern Ukraine and Russia began to arrive in Europe, some of them just for a time, like Attila's Huns, and others more permanently, like the Magyars, the people who are today's Hungarians.

Much of the contact and trade people from outside Finland had with the Finns occurred in what is called Finland Proper (*Varsinais-Suomi* in Finnish). Finland Proper is the territory on the other side of the Åland Islands from Sweden and includes today's city of Turku. It had been home to most of the Finnish population for centuries. During the Migration Period, groups of Finns began to move eastward along the coast of the Gulf of Finland to the location of modern Helsinki.

Finland is much colder than most other European countries, but it is warmed to a degree by the currents of the Baltic Sea. The southern coasts are a bit more protected from harsh weather, so temperatures there are a bit higher on average. This means that while the southern coast of Finland is not as fertile as California's Central Valley, more varieties and more plentiful crops will grow there than in other parts of the country.

One of the more noteworthy things about the Migration Period and the end of the Roman Period in Finland was the growth in the use and production of iron. The Iron Age came later to Finland, but evidence of domestic iron production has been found that dates to the Migration Period. Additionally, the swords, axes, and knives found by archaeologists in Finland clearly show the influence of the Germanic cultures bordering Finland to the west and south.

The Early Middle Ages or the Merovingian Period

The Merovingians were the ruling dynasty in today's France from the mid-400s to the rise of the Carolingians (the dynasty that included Charlemagne) in 751. The term has nothing to do with Finland in any way; it's simply a term used by historians to indicate different periods of time.

During the Merovingian Period, Finland imported more and more goods from other nations. With a couple of exceptions over the course of 250-plus years, that meant traders came to Finland, not the other way around. Some of the more valuable items were weapons that were far beyond Finnish skills at the time. Many of these weapons were not only stronger than what the Finns made at home but were also more decorative as well, which indicates what historians have believed for some time: that Finland, much like its Nordic neighbors of Sweden and Norway, was divided into a group of small kingdoms. The remains of wooden hillforts, partially preserved by the cold weather or protected by the bogs and lakes of the country, also indicate a tribal culture consisting of various petty kingdoms.

Like the Swedes and the Norwegians, the Finnish kingdoms likely traded, formed alliances, and battled each other at different times.

One of the other important changes taking place in Finland, at least to a small degree, was the arrival of Christianity. Archaeologists have found a number of graves with Christian grave goods near the village of Orismala on the central western coast of the Gulf of Bothnia that date from the late Merovingian Period. This does not mean that most or even many Finns were Christian at the time, but it is another indicator of Finnish contact with the outside world. You'll learn more about native Finnish spiritual beliefs shortly.

Chapter 2 – Vikings?

Finnish tourists traveling in the United States or elsewhere likely have had the following conversation before:

"Hi, where are you from?"

"Finland."

"Oh, you're a Viking!"

Finns hear this more often than they would care to. People with Scandinavian heritage might think having ancestors who were Vikings is kind of cool. But remember, Finns are not Scandinavians, and they're definitely not Swedes, which was the nearest Viking civilization to Finland in the Viking Age.

However, while Finns, as a whole, were not Vikings, there were individuals and small groups of Finns that were. Although all of the people of Scandinavia during the Viking Age (793–1066) are sometimes described as Vikings, this is usually done for the convenience of the writer and is usually preceded by a disclaimer that says something like "Though not all Scandinavians were Vikings, we occasionally use the term to describe the people of Scandinavia as a whole." This is acceptable, but it is not really correct. Vikings were not an ethnic group. Vikings were mostly men who banded together to raid, war, and trade with the people of Europe during the Viking Age. Many Scandinavians (Norwegians, Swedes, Danes, and Icelanders) were not Vikings; they were farmers, fishermen, and blacksmiths.

Additionally, while most people who "went Viking" were Scandinavian, not all of them were. In Ireland, a new Hiberno-Norse culture began sometime after the Viking raids commenced in Britain and Ireland (Hibernia was the Roman name for Ireland). The same thing occurred to a degree in Scotland, especially on the coast of the Irish Sea. Additionally, men who sought adventure and were trusted by the Scandinavians as traders or allies could become Vikings. We know there were Frisian/Dutch Vikings and German Vikings. Later in the period, a new Viking culture was born out of the Swedes' adventures in Russia and Ukraine.

So, were there Finnish Vikings? Yes. We know this because a peace treaty between the Vikings of Kievan Rus' and the Byzantine Empire (Eastern Roman Empire) in 945 includes three Finnish names side by side with the Swedish ones. So, while there were Finnish Vikings (at least three of them), the vast majority of Finns were not.

Vikings and Finns

We know that the Vikings and Finns had contact. The location of Finland alone tells us they must have had contact, but other records (including Scandinavian Viking Age goods in Finland) tell us they did.

Because both Viking and Finnish cultures were pre-literate people with no contemporary written histories at the time, we know very little about the contact between the two groups of people. We know a bit about the contact between the Finns and the Vikings, mostly Swedish Vikings. Although assumption is not good historical practice, it's likely that the contact between the Finns and Vikings was similar to the Vikings' contact with other people in Europe and beyond.

In central Sweden, there is an island called Birka. During the Viking Age, the land and waterways were much different than they are now because of erosion and climate changes. Birka was one of the biggest international trading posts in Europe at the time. Goods from China, the Middle East, the Mediterranean, and elsewhere were bought, sold, and bartered for at Birka.

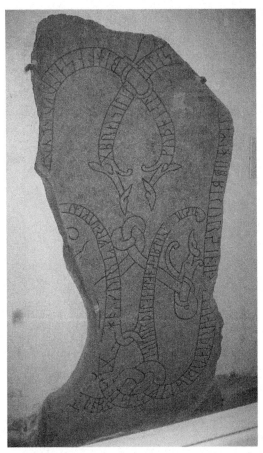

Runestone Gs-13 found in Sweden north of Stockholm. It mentions the death of a man named Brusi, who was killed in battle in central Finland. The carvings also indicate that Brusi was a Christian. It is dated to c. 1000.

Finns may have gone to Birka to trade and later may have traveled to the island of Gotland, which succeeded Birka as the main Swedish trading station after the waterways to Birka silted up. We don't have much evidence of Finns outside of Finland, Estonia, and a small part of northern Russia, so it may be that the Finns counted on people coming to them with goods. We know that the Finns likely traded for weapons and other goods, probably rare luxury items like glass or fine jewelry. The Finns traded or sold furs, amber, and ivory, some of which they may have traded for with the Sami people, who still inhabit parts of northern Scandinavia and Finland.

Iron Age swords found in Finland. The same style of sword has been found in all areas inhabited or visited by the Vikings.

Swords in similar styles from earlier times and in greater numbers have been found in the Viking homelands and in places they visited, so it's highly likely that these weapons originated with the Northmen. Additionally, the sites in Finland where these swords were found are near coastlines, not inland, which would indicate contact between Vikings and Finns in Finland itself. Scandinavians also sailed to Finland to trade. Given human nature and what we know about the Vikings, it's likely that the Vikings brought slaves to Finland to sell or trade and probably took Finnish slaves as well.

Finland was a collection of tribal kingdoms and clan alliances. Given what we know about Viking Age societies throughout Europe, it seems likely that some Vikings took Finnish slaves from areas where they had not established trade connections. They probably sold enslaved Finns from one area to another region or a rival kingdom.

There are a number of stories handed down through the centuries about conflicts between the Finns and the Vikings. Many of these come from Finland and are a bit light on the details. Others are written in the sagas. The vast majority of the sagas do not mention Finland at all.

What could be the reasons for the dearth of information regarding Viking Age ties between the Scandinavians and Finns? We can make a couple of educated guesses.

First, there is no record of Finnish warships or any kind of large ship during the Viking era, although they did have boats. None of the neighboring people who were victimized by the Vikings mention raids by the Finns. So, aside from the relatively few Finns who joined Viking bands, like those in the attack on the Byzantine Empire circa 945, most of the contact between Finns and Vikings probably happened in Finland.

This contact also likely happened on the coast. This would have given the Vikings an escape route if they needed to flee. Additionally, many of the larger and richer Finnish settlements were by the ocean. Finland's coast also had much more visibility, generally speaking, than the heavily forested interior. Aside from making movement difficult, the Vikings would have been at a decided disadvantage in any battle that took place in the forest, not because they couldn't fight there but because the Finns knew the forests like the back of their hand. They knew the best place for an ambush, concealment, and camps.

One of the stories that come to us via the sagas is the story of Agne and Skjalf. The story is told in the *Yngling saga*, which was written by Snorri Sturluson, the Icelandic warrior and poet of the late 12th and early 13th centuries. The *Yngling saga* tells of the creation of the universe, Earth, and the Norse gods. It also includes stories from the first kings of Scandinavia. Many of these tales have to be taken with a grain of salt, though.

According to Snorri, there was an ancient Swedish king named Agne. Like most kings in ancient times, Agne was a warrior. While on a raid to Finland, he killed a Finnish chieftain named Froste. (One of the interesting things about the Finns mentioned in the saga is that they have Scandinavian names. Those either came down to Snorri like that, or he changed them from Finnish to Swedish-sounding names for his audience.)

Froste's son Loge and daughter Skjalf were taken prisoner by Agne, and the Swedish king fell in love with Skjalf. She agreed to marry him but told the king that he would first have to hold a funeral feast for her father that involved great quantities of beer. At the feast, Agne began to drink heavily, and Skjalf asked to see the gold he had taken from her father. This gold must have been in the form of necklaces and torques (more like a heavy decorative collar than a necklace), for Agne put the gold around his neck. He paraded around to show his new wealth before passing out.

While he was unconscious, Skjalf tied a rope to the back of the jewelry and had her Finnish compatriots hoist the king in a tree, where he hanged and suffocated. Then Skjalf and her men stole a boat and sailed away. Snorri says that Agne was killed somewhere south of Stockholm. Legend has it that he was buried in an area near Stockholm called Sollentuna, near where the modern train station stands.

Skjalf having King Agne hanged. Engraving by Hugo Hamilton, 1830.
https://commons.wikimedia.org/wiki/File:Konung_Agne_blir_om_natten_upph%C3%A4ngd_i_ett_tr%C3%A4d_by_Hugo_Hamilton.jpg

There are a number of other myths, legends, and rumors about the Finns and Vikings or, rather, how the Vikings saw the Finns. Many of them have to do with the Vikings' fear of the deep Finnish forests and lakes. Add to the trepidation anyone feels in an unfamiliar land, especially one where people want to do you harm, was the idea that the Finns were adept spell-casters. They could supposedly make men see things that weren't there, conjure spirits that would get them lost in the forest, and change the weather. There is a story that the Vikings did not want to take Finns on raids because the Finns could control the weather, which would put the Vikings at their mercy.

All of this is understandable. Since time began, men have been attributing supernatural powers to their enemies. Why? Well, if the enemy is vanquished, then you've defeated a powerful enemy with magical powers, causing your status as a warrior or leader to go up. If you lose, then it wasn't because you're a bad warrior; it's just that you are up against an enemy who has magic.

Since Swedish settlements on the Åland Islands and the coast of Finland began during the Viking era, we can assume that many of the conflicts, whether they were military, political, or both, went to the Vikings.

However, we do know of one battle that was won by the Finns, who forced the famous King Olaf of Norway (r. c. 995–1028) to flee. Olaf, who was one of the first Viking chieftains in a Scandinavian country to convert to Christianity and was made a saint by the Catholic Church after his death at the Battle of Stiklestad, is one of the most famous Vikings described in Snorri Sturluson's saga *Heimskringla*. In the following excerpt, you can learn about many aspects of the Vikings and what little we know of the Finns:

"After this they sailed to Finland and plundered there, and went up the country. All the people fled to the forest, and they had emptied their houses of all household goods. The king went far up the country, and through some woods, and came to some dwellings in a valley called Herdaler, where, however, they made but small booty, and saw no people; and as it was getting late in the day, the king turned back to his ships. Now when they came into the woods again people rushed upon them from all quarters, and made a severe attack. The king told his men to cover themselves with their shields, but before they got out of the woods he lost many people, and many were wounded; but at last, late in the evening, he got to the ships. The Finlanders conjured up in the night, by their witchcraft, a dreadful storm and bad weather on the sea; but the king ordered the anchors to be weighed and sail hoisted, and beat off all night to the outside of the land. The king's luck prevailed more than the Finlanders' witchcraft; for he had the luck to beat round the Balagard's side in the night. and so got out to sea. But the Finnish army proceeded on land, making the same progress as the king made with his ships. So says Sigvat:

'The third fight was at Herdaler, where
The men of Finland met in war
The hero of the royal race,
With ringing sword-blades face to face.
Off Balagard's shore the waves
Ran hollow; but the sea-king saves
His hard-pressed ship, and gains the lee
Of the east coast through the wild sea.'"

In 2008 and 2010, archaeologists recovered two vessels that were built in the years just before the Viking Age began. These two boats were not the traditional Viking dragon ships but rather precursors to them. They were powered by oars and showed some of the characteristics of later Viking sailing ships.

The boats were found near the village of Salma on the Estonian island of Saaremaa, which lies only a short distance from the mainland. The boats held forty-one bodies, which were placed in orderly rows after their deaths, which were violent. Both boats were burial vessels, and they carried all the earmarks of a Scandinavian burial. We don't know who their enemies were. They might have been other Vikings or people from mainland Europe not indigenous to the island, but it's just as likely, perhaps even more so, that the Vikings' enemy on Saaremaa were Finns or their related Estonian cousins, who speak a closely related language and still trade with Finland.

In the later part of the Viking Age, existent records from 1042 tell of attacks on Finland by the Viking Rus' king of Novgorod, Vladimir Yaroslavich, whose father was Russian and mother Swedish.

A birchbark manuscript dating from the late 11th or early 12th century tells of attacks in Karelia (parts of which lay in modern-day Finland and Russia) by the Lithuanians between the years 1060 and 1080. At the time, the Lithuanians were a growing regional power.

Drawing of a birchbark manuscript in Finnish runes, the earliest known use of a written Finnish language.

https://commons.wikimedia.org/wiki/File:Birch-bark_letter_292.gif

Chapter 3 – The *Kalevala*

Now we're going to skip from what we know about early Finnish history to the 19th century but only to tell you about some important work done by one of the most influential men in Finnish history, though he is not a household name by any means, at least outside Finland.

His name was Elias Lönnrot. He was born in the village of Sammatti near the coast of south-central Finland in 1802 and died there in 1884. During his long life, Lönnrot and many other Finns read about the explosion of national feelings in Europe following the French Revolutions of 1789 and 1848.

Lönnrot in 1872 by Bernhard Reinhold.
https://commons.wikimedia.org/wiki/File:Elias_L%C3%B6nnrot_by_Reinhold.jpeg

Europeans had previously thought of themselves as subjects of one monarch or another, even rulers who were foreigners. The people slowly began to identify more with their ethnic and cultural roots than with a monarchy under which they had little, if any, say.

As you will learn in the following chapter, Finland was part of the Swedish Empire for centuries. Though there had been local rebellions against Swedish rule at times, these were sporadic and generally not supported by the entire Finnish population. However, by the time Elias Lönnrot began studying the evolution of the Finnish language and the oral traditions of Finland, there was an increasing sense that the Finns were losing their history and that the country, especially in the south and southwest, was becoming more "Swedish" in its culture, language, and politics. Finnish was looked down upon by ethnic Swedish, Finnish, and Finno-Swedish elites as the language of the peasants and uneducated.

During Lönnrot's lifetime, he made many trips to the more remote regions of Finland, especially in the lands of the Sami people in the central and far northern parts of the country and the Karelia region on the border with Russia. He talked to as many people as he could about the stories that had been told from one generation to the next. Many of the different groups of people Lönnrot spoke with were illiterate. However, like in other pre-literate and tribal societies, Sami and Finnish storytellers had memorized the stories of their ancestors.

Lönnrot traveled through Finland beginning in 1827 and continued making long journeys into the hinterlands for over thirty years. While writing down the many stories he was told, Lönnrot also had time to put together a guide to Finnish plant life in the Finnish language. Later in life, he compiled and published the first Finnish-Swedish dictionary.

But it is the collection of stories and epic poems that he gathered from the Sami and others that Elias Lönnrot is most famous for. This is the *Kalevala*, the epic poem of Finland. Because of the *Kalevala*, we have a basic knowledge of what the ancient Finns believed about the world, the universe, the gods, and the afterlife.

When Lönnrot sat down through the years to study, organize, and transpose his notes into a sensible and somewhat chronological account, he realized there were significant gaps and even contradictions in many of the stories he had been told. This is not surprising, considering that before Lönnrot, the stories that eventually made up the *Kalevala* were part of an oral tradition going back nearly one thousand years, perhaps more.

For many reasons, including readability, Lönnrot filled in the gaps with his best guesses and what he believed the people of earlier times might have believed. This means that the *Kalevala* is partially the product of Lönnrot's imagination, although it is still an important piece of Finnish history. Still, it makes for an entertaining read and forms the basis for modern ideas about the Finnish spirit world, creation myth, and gods. The gods and heroes of the Finns have similarities and differences with the famous Norse gods of Finland's Scandinavian neighbors.

Like many creation myths, the Finnish version begins with something already in existence, in this case, a giant bird whose egg forms the roof of the sky. Inside this half of an eggshell is the flat earth, and the sky revolves around the top of the shell, which is anchored on the North Star. Coming straight down from the North Star was an invisible energy field, imagined as a sort of "stellar whirlpool," which also served as a conduit for the souls of the dead. The souls would travel through this magical whirlpool of stars into the land of the dead, Tuonela.

At the edges of the flat earth was not a void, like many ancients believed, but another land that people could not journey to. This land was the land of the birds or Lintukoto, a warm paradise where many birds went during the winter. Today, the skies of rural Finland are almost as free from ambient light as they were centuries ago. On a clear night, it is very easy to see the Milky Way, the bright band of stars that marks the center of our galaxy as seen from Earth. The Milky Way was called Linnunrata ("the path of the birds") by the Finns, as it was believed to be the path migrating birds used to travel from Earth to Lintukoto. Incidentally, the word *lintukoto* is used by Finns today to mean a place like paradise, a place where you might want to vacation during the long northern winter, like Tahiti, for example.

The Milky Way as seen from northern Chile.
Bruno Gilli/ESO, CC BY 4.0 <https://creativecommons.org/licenses/by/4.0>, via Wikimedia Commons, https://commons.wikimedia.org/w/index.php?curid=11657991

Animal spirits play a large part in traditional Finnish stories, particularly birds, who were believed to bring the soul to a human being at birth and to Tuonela at death. An invisible bird, the Sielulintu, stood vigil by a person when they slept, making sure the soul did not wander off during dreams.

The bear was considered the most powerful and revered animal and spirit, so much so that it was barely called by its proper name, *karhu*. Bears were seen as the living embodiment of ancestors and were called by other names, such as *otso* ("browed one") or *kontio* ("land dweller").

Gods and Heroes

Bears and birds were not gods, though they were sometimes depicted as supernatural. No, the gods were superhuman, and for the most part, they were depicted much like any other pagan god: muscular heroes, powerful old men, and very beautiful or very ugly women.

The most powerful of the gods was Ukko, the god of the sky and thunder. In this way, he was similar to Thor, the Norse god of thunder. However, unlike Thor, Ukko was an old man, though he did possess a stone hammer. Ukko is sometimes equated with another name, Ilmarinen, the god of thunder and blacksmiths, who is one of the main characters of the *Kalevala*. Ilmarinen and Ukko are often considered one and the same, though the name Ukko is more recent. *Ukkonen* is the Finnish word for "thunder."

In the *Kalevala*, Ilmarinen/Ukko is credited with creating the stars and making the most treasured object in the Finnish supernatural universe: the Sampo. The Sampo is a magical object that granted its holder riches and good fortune. The Sampo is created by Ilmarinen for the witch Louhi, who promises the blacksmith her beautiful daughter's hand in marriage if he can make something that will ensure her bright future. When Louhi sees the power of the Sampo for the first time, she devises a plan to steal it. After it is stolen, Ilmarinen's land and people begin to suffer. A large portion of the *Kalevala* tells of Ilmarinen's journey to recover his magical object, but it gets smashed during a battle at sea and is lost forever in the depths of the ocean.

Ilmarinen is joined on his voyage by the most famous ancient Finnish hero, Väinämöinen, who is depicted as an older, wise man who is still physically strong. What's more, he possesses a magical voice and instrument, his kantele (a combination between a harp and a lyre), which he uses to bewitch people, especially beautiful women. His voice is so powerful that he can create things with it, such as the boat he uses to sail off into the sunset at the end of the *Kalevala* after he is defeated by an especially intelligent newborn baby who chides the hero for all of his sins. Before Väinämöinen leaves the shores of the mortal world, he vows to return someday to help humanity by singing a new golden age into existence.

Obviously, the story of Väinämöinen's end presages the arrival of Christianity in Finland, and it may be that Lönnrot created the ending himself. For a time, it was thought that Lönnrot may have made up about half of the *Kalevala*, but recent studies indicate that only about 3 percent of the story can be attributed to Lönnrot's imagination. About 14 percent of the stories are compilations that he made from a variety of similar stories. The rest are mostly unchanged, except for readability and organization.

The *Kalevala* contains many more stories than just Ilmarinen's creation of the Sampo and Väinämöinen's singing. Many more heroes and villains, both otherworldly and mortal, are described within it, as are many goddesses and beautiful maidens, witches, and magical creatures.

The *Kalevala* has influenced Finns since its publication, most notably in the works of Finland's most famous composer, Jean Sibelius (1865–1957). February 28th is a national holiday and is known both as Finnish Culture Day and Kalevala Day.

Väinämöinen playing his kantele.

Chapter 4 – The Swedish Crusades

Most Swedes had converted to Christianity by the early 1100s. For the most part, the conversion of Sweden from a pagan to a Christian society was smoother and more gradual than it was in neighboring Norway, where pagan earls and peasant rebellions violently resisted Christianization for some time.

The Danish king (more of a powerful clan chieftain) Harald Klak had converted to Christianity in 826, but this was likely done under duress, as he was in exile in France at the time. When he returned to Denmark to seize the throne, he was supported by the king of the Franks, Louis the Pious, and returned to Denmark with an important but little-known figure of Scandinavian history, the Frankish monk Ansgar. However, Ansgar's missionary work would have to wait, for Harald Klak was defeated in his attempt to seize the Danish throne. Harald became a feared and infamous pirate, raiding the northern coasts of Europe, including France. He also appears to have given Christianity lip service and likely went back to his old beliefs.

The first Danish king to become a Christian was Harald Bluetooth, who agreed to be baptized in 965. However, this was likely only done so he could establish better trade relations with the kingdoms to his south and prevent an invasion by the more powerful Franks.

It would be another half-century before the kings of Norway converted to the new religion, and the Catholic Church would not found bishoprics there until about 1100, establishing both religious and secular ties with the ruling classes in Norway. With the coming of Christianity and the defeat of the Vikings in England at Stamford Bridge in 1066, the Viking Age came to an end, but that did not mean the Swedes were done invading other countries. Now, they invaded other countries to convert pagans to Christianity.

The three Swedish Crusades occurred circa 1155, 1239, and 1293. But before we tell you more about these events, you should know a bit more about Ansgar, the monk. Ansgar was from Bremen, the famous northwestern German port. He was given the task of spreading the gospel in Scandinavia and arrived at the famous Swedish trading station of Birka in 829, three years after his adventures with Harald Klak.

Ansgar did not convert many people at the famous trading post, but he did make important inroads for his faith by attracting rich and influential converts, like the local king's steward and a wealthy widow and noblewoman Mor Frideborg, who, in addition to being one of the first Swedish converts, is also the first woman in Swedish history whose identity can be confirmed from historical documents.

In 831, Ansgar became the bishop of Bremen, and between dealing with secular political matters and converting northern Germans and the Danes (who raided the Christian city of Hamburg and destroyed church records and relics), he did not return to Sweden until sometime between 848 and 850. Once there, he managed to avert a violent pagan reaction to Christianity. In 854, Ansgar returned to Sweden and joined the court of the powerful chieftain at Birka, Olof, who is said to have been favorably disposed toward the new faith.

Ansgar taught the rudiments of the Christian faith and educated and converted many Swedes. By the time of his death in Germany in 865, Christianity had a foothold in Sweden, though it would take another 150 years or so for most Swedes to embrace the new religion. The last pagan Swedish king was Blot-Sweyn, who reigned for three years, from 1084 to 1087.

Sixty-three years after the death of Blot-Sweyn, Swedish King Erik IX (also known as Erik the Saint or Erik the Holy) began the First

Swedish Crusade into Finland. By the time of Erik's reign, Christianity had not only become the spiritual belief system of most Swedes but also a political ideology. The basis of this ideology was that, at least in theory, the unification of all people under Christ would lead to peace and, more importantly, would hasten the Second Coming, in which Jesus would return to Earth and usher in everlasting peace, prosperity, and happiness. But many believed that in order for that to happen, the gospel had to be spread to all corners of the world. The Swedes decided to begin with Finland, but religion was not the only reason they moved into the southern and western coasts of Finland beginning in 1155.

The First Swedish Crusade might not have even happened. Missionary activity had been growing in Finland, with missionaries coming from Sweden and Novgorod, which eventually grew into Russia. The Swedes, like the Norwegians and Danes, were Catholic. The Russians were Eastern Orthodox. To a degree, over the next two centuries, these two sects of Christianity would struggle to claim Finland for their respective churches. When we refer to a "crusade" in Finland, we are talking about a much more gradual one. This crusade was performed mostly by monks and Swedish nobility rather than armies of men forcibly converting the Finns. That would come later.

From the time of Charlemagne onward, power and influence in much of Europe east of the Rhine River were fought over by various popes and the Holy Roman emperors. Though, in theory, the emperor was subservient to the pope and the church, stronger and richer emperors had more power than the pope in Rome. This struggle was mostly peaceful, though it wasn't always. The pope was a secular leader as well, and he was able to field sizable armies at times because of the church's massive treasury.

What's more, though the emperors and popes had been playing political games for hundreds of years, most of these intrigues played out in mainland Europe. In other words, their conflicts did not take place in the Nordic countries. Norway, Sweden, and Finland were wide open as far as the church and emperors were concerned, and they attempted to fill the void.

The Swedes were moving toward a unified kingdom under one monarch rather than having tribal chieftains or petty kings of smaller areas. To counter the complete consolidation of power in the hands of the Swedish kings and to counter the influence of the archbishopric of Bremen in Germany, which controlled the churches of southern Sweden and was more loyal to the emperor than the pope, the church established archbishoprics in Lund and Uppsala, Sweden.

That left Finland. Across the Baltic from Finland are the modern-day countries of Lithuania, Latvia, and Estonia. There were two Holy Roman emperors for most of the 12th century: Conrad III (r. 1138–1152) and Frederick I "Barbarossa" (r. 1155–1190). These two rulers forcibly carried Christianity into the Baltic region, sometimes with great violence. The pope rightly expected that the emperors would make an effort to convert the Finns and secure their loyalty. If this happened, almost the entire northern coast of Europe would be more loyal to (or afraid of) the emperor than the papacy.

In the 1100s, the struggles for power among those who wanted to be king of Sweden allowed the popes to play one man against another while still being at the forefront of establishing a greater presence in Finland.

The leader of the missionary effort in Finland was a British monk named Henry. Henry was backed by one of the most powerful Swedish kings in history, King Erik of the Svear. The missionary work and conversion of the Finns, particularly on the western and southern coasts, went relatively smoothly, but that "easy" effort didn't quite fit in with the narrative the church wanted people to believe. A better story is that Henry, despite many troubles and much violence, managed not only to firmly establish the church but also carried out miracles while he did so.

After his death, Henry became Saint Henrik, the patron saint of the new Catholic diocese of Åbo (present-day Turku). Henry's death was one of the violent instances that marred the mostly peaceful growth of the church in Finland in the 1100s. He was murdered in his new diocese, or at least that's the legend. Finnish history records many different versions of Henry's death, with most of them involving a peasant named Lalli.

Bishop Henry killed by Lalli, Romantic-era painting by Albert Edelfelt
https://commons.wikimedia.org/w/index.php?curid=16348922

Power Struggles over Finland between the 12th and 14th Centuries

The First Swedish Crusade was launched in the name of religion, but much of what occurred in 1155 was part of a power struggle between the pope and the Holy Roman emperors.

Over the next two centuries, religion was used as a convenient cover for additional plots and power moves involving Sweden, Finland, Denmark (which was an economic and military power to reckon with at the time), and the growing strength of Novgorod. The Germanic Hanseatic League, a collection of wealthy and powerful cities, was also a major player in the struggle to control parts of Finland and the Baltic. Obtaining Finland would give a nation (or league) a strategic advantage because of its coastline, especially in the far south and southwest. A great deal of trade sailed in and out of the eastern Baltic and the Gulf of Finland, and whichever kingdom controlled the coastlines could control trade by denying ports to competitors and charging exorbitant port fees and transit taxes.

The coastlines of the Baltic countries were also contested, and in 1219, the Danes founded the port of Reval, which is now Tallinn, the capital of Estonia. In Estonian (again, a language related to Finnish), *Taani linn* means "town of the Danes." Strangely, though the Estonians later called it the "town of the Danes," most of the foreigners there were German Hanseatic traders, who would soon, with the tacit approval of the Swedes, begin to move into the villages, towns, and growing cities in Turku and the southern coasts. In both Sweden and Finland, German traders wielded considerable influence, and their power would last until it was finally controlled to a great degree by the great unifying Swedish king, Gustav I Vasa, in the 1500s.

In 1240 and 1242, two of the most famous battles in history, or at least in Russian history, took place. Prince Alexander of Novgorod defeated an army of Swedes at the Neva River, which would run through the city of St. Petersburg when it was founded in 1703 under Tsar Peter the Great. Prince Alexander is known to history as Alexander Nevsky for his victory on the Neva. This victory helped contain Swedish expansion in Finland, and much of the eastern part of the country remained Eastern Orthodox (the faith of the Russians) until relatively recently. Somewhere in the neighborhood of just 1 to 2 percent of Finns today are Eastern Orthodox, and most of them live in the eastern borderlands of the country, closest to Russia.

Despite the defeat inflicted by Alexander Nevsky (who also defeated the famous Teutonic Knights in Estonia in 1242, giving Novgorod greater influence in the Baltic), the Swedes were the major political and military power in Finland. In both Sweden and Finland, the church and the increasingly powerful kings of the Svear began to centralize power in Sweden and Finland under their control.

Sweden, at least the Sweden we know today, was not completely Swedish in the 13th century. In actuality, much of the lower part of the country, especially toward the west across the straits from Denmark, was under the control of the Danes. In many places in the area, the Danes outnumbered the Swedes. The Danes controlled the area directly through Danish princes and nobles allied with the Danish Crown and indirectly through Hanseatic German traders allied with Denmark and Swedes from the south, who often identified more with the Danes than their fellow Swedes. On top of all that, many of the southern Swedes wanted to rule all of Sweden and were not keen on seeing northern and tribal rivals consolidate power at their expense.

Though the Danes in Denmark and what is now southern Sweden wanted greater influence and trade in Finland, the Swedes would dominate Finland because of Sweden's location to Finland and the northern Swedish kings and the church (with its riches) holding centralized power in their hands.

One reason the Swedes were able to control parts of Finland was that it was sparsely populated. Aside from the Swedish far north, Finland is generally much colder and more forested. Additionally, away from the coasts, the land is much less arable than in Sweden. This meant the Finnish population was smaller than Sweden and Denmark, as it is today. The land and climate would not allow a large population at the time due to their crude understanding of agriculture and medicine.

The Swedes were able to move into western Finland with relative ease, and the colonization was not, for the most part, hostile. Finns and Swedes lived in relative harmony. Still, at the first signs of Swedish penetration into new parts of Finland (in the south and west), many Finnish tribal leaders and their people cleared and marked new areas of somewhat arable land for themselves.

It made sense for the Swedes to get along with their Finnish neighbors, even though the Finns were sparsely populated and in the minority. Though the Swedes could count on their king to strike back against any hostile act, Sweden and the forts containing Swedish troops were few and far between. Due to the difficult landscape and climate, traveling by horse was not much faster than walking. Any Swedish settlers who angered enough Finns in the countryside would be on their own.

World history is full of stories about colonizers conquering people in violent conflicts. In Finland, with few exceptions, the gradual colonization of the country, which started in the southwest and moved slowly toward the area of the modern capital, Helsinki, was peaceful. By the mid-14th century, the closeness of the Finns and Swedes resulted in the merging of cultures. By the 15th century, what historians call "Fenno-Swedish culture" emerged, which included elements of both. Many Finns and Swedes in the south and western coastal areas could speak one another's language, though more Finns learned to speak Swedish than the other way around.

The Second Swedish Crusade

In 1239, a Swedish nobleman and contender for a unified Sweden, Birger Jarl, led an expedition into the hinterlands of south-central Finland, a land called "Tavastland." The people there, known (unsurprisingly) as the Tavasts, rose up in rebellion against the Catholic Church, declared themselves Orthodox, and had been establishing close ties with Novgorod. With the blessing of the Church, Birger Jarl led a punitive expedition against the Tavasts. He put down the rebellion and built a castle in Tavastland to help keep order and administer the area in the name of Sweden. With the support of the church, the Swedes made Finland (or what they controlled of it at the time) a part of their kingdom in 1250 under King Valdemar. Swedish rule of Finland would continue for over five hundred years.

The Third Swedish Crusade

In 1293, the Swedes sought to expand their political and military power to other parts of Finland, namely Karelia, the area that borders modern Russia today. As you learned just a moment ago, most Karelians were Orthodox. Additionally, a small number were still pagan, at least partially. For religious and financial reasons, the Catholic Church wished to expand into Orthodox Karelia, and the Swedish nobility wished to enlarge the area under their control, especially at the expense of Russia, which had been growing its influence in the area. Another reason, at least according to the Swedish King Birger Magnusson, was that the Karelians preyed on trade missions and held Swedish hostages, most of whom were tortured and killed. A band of Karelians had also trekked to Sweden and carried out a raid in 1257, which cost many lives.

The conversion of the Karelians was not as peaceful as what had occurred earlier in other parts of the country. Leaders of Karelian tribes were burned at the stake and subjected to many unpleasant punishments; the Middle Ages is famous for torture.

The leader of the Swedish expedition, a Swedish noble and constable of the realm named Torgils (Torkel) Knutsson, built a fortress in the town of Viborg on the Karelian Isthmus, just north of present-day St. Petersburg. (Viborg was the Swedish name for the town. Viipuri was the Finnish name. Vyborg is its Russian name, and Russia has owned the territory since the end of the Winter War in 1940).

The establishment of a permanent Swedish settlement in Viborg helped to pacify the Karelian region and place Sweden firmly in charge of Finland. The Treaty of Nöteborg (1323) settled the border between Novgorod and Sweden and also marked the recognized demarcation point between Catholicism and Orthodoxy. The Third

Swedish Crusade and the Treaty of Nöteborg are immensely important to Finnish history. The treaty brought Finland into Catholic western Europe. For the most part, Finnish culture, economy, and language (remember, Swedish is one of the official languages of Finland, and until the end of WWI, the sizable and wealthy Swedish minority wielded great power in Finland). When Russia took control of Finland in 1809, it took control of an almost completely Westernized country. For much of the time that Russia "owned" Finland, it gave the Finns freedom in their own affairs that no other territory in the Russian Empire enjoyed. That did not mean that Russian rule was benign; at times, especially after the installation of a particularly brutal governor, it could be oppressive.

By the early 16th century, the Swedes had built a number of large fortresses and castles of various sizes to control and administer the country. Near each of these castles and fortresses were the expanding diocese and archdiocese of the church. Together, the church and the Swedish Crown (which would become even more powerful with the rise of King Gustav I Vasa in the 1520s) would establish firm control over all of Finland.

Pagans

In Iceland, remnants of the old Norse beliefs still remain. Elves, gnomes, and other spirits are believed by many Icelanders to actually exist, at least sometimes. Similarly, aspects of old pagan beliefs still exist in Finland, as you saw with the word for thunder.

You may know that the Christmas tree has absolutely nothing to do with Christianity. Historians differ in their belief about the origin of the tradition of a lighted tree but suffice it to say that the holiday tree was a pagan tradition that was subsumed by Christians in later centuries. Same with the Yule log, with "Yule" being an Old Norse word. In Finland and other parts of Europe, the most obvious example of the church adjusting to "heathen" practices was the fertility rites that took place in the spring. Though the sexual aspect of the pagan rites was eliminated, the symbolic sacrifices made during the rites were changed slightly into the Catholic holiday of Whitsun, the marking of the ascension of Christ and the birth of the Catholic Church. In Finland, Whitsun became an excuse to party, just like in pagan times.

Chapter 5 – Gustav I Vasa and the Reformation

"The Father of Modern Sweden," King Gustav I Vasa, 1542
https://commons.wikimedia.org/w/index.php?curid=73305

In 1397, the Danes, Norwegians, and Swedes formed one of the earliest formal multi-national states, the Kalmar Union, named after the town in which it was officially proclaimed. In 2022, Finland, Sweden, and Estonia were all led by women, and from 1397 until 1412, the Kalmar Union was ruled by a woman, the powerful and often-overlooked Margaret I of Denmark.

Though the Kalmar Union was relatively strong under Margaret, after her death, the relatively poor economies, small populations, and internal political and ethnic strife meant that, though the union still existed in name, it grew slowly weaker after Margaret's death. However, many Danish kings still asserted their over-lordship over both Sweden and Norway. Though there were many reasons for the growing weakness of the Kalmar Union after Margaret, two of them involved Sweden directly.

First, the Danes continued to hold the southern part of Sweden. They had for centuries, but as the 16th century approached, common geography, strategies, and ethnicity compelled generations of Swedish kings and nobles, especially those from the north-central part of the country, to try and either maneuver or force the Danes out. Economically, Swedish rule of the southern part of the country would allow them to have some control over the commercial traffic passing through the straits that separated Sweden from Europe.

Second, the Danes used their position in southern Sweden to interfere in the country's politics. The Danes supported a variety of candidates for the Swedish throne, contributing to political, economic, and ethnic instability. The Danes also encouraged the settlement of rich German Hanseatic traders in many of the cities, ports, and castles of southern Sweden, which, over the centuries, became a very important issue in the struggle to unify all of Sweden under one powerful king. At that time, Sweden would have included all of what we know as Sweden today and much else, including Finland.

The man who eventually united the Swedes and established a dynasty that would drive the Danes completely out of Sweden in 1658 was Gustav I Vasa. (The Swedes have a unique method for their royal titles. In this case, Gustav was the man's first name; he was the first "Gustav" to rule Sweden. His last name was "Vasa." Today's Swedish king is Karl XVI Gustaf. He is the sixteenth Karl, and Gustaf is his middle name, not the name of the ruling family. His family can trace its lineage back to Jean Bernadotte, one of Napoleon's marshals who was asked by the Swedes to take the throne in 1818.)

In 1520, growing Swedish power was a threat to the Danish king (who ruled Denmark and the Kalmar Union), Kristian II. That year, Kristian invaded Stockholm to put down a growing rebellion against his rule among the Swedish nobility. When he arrived in Stockholm, he invited the leading Swedish nobles to dinner and then had them arrested on trumped-up and complicated charges of heresy. Eighty-two men were executed shortly thereafter. One of them was the father of Gustav Vasa, who was traveling in disguise through the Hanseatic cities of northern Germany at the time.

When Gustav returned to Sweden, much of the southern countryside and coast that weren't already under Danish control had fallen to King Kristian, but many of the cities, like Stockholm and Uppsala, remained in Swedish hands, as did the central part of the country, where Vasa's family was from and where they were strongest. When Vasa returned, he raised an army and began a war against the Danes, which resulted in him becoming king of all of Sweden, except for the small Danish holdings on the southern coast, which were eventually made Swedish in 1658.

Gustav Vasa is considered the Father of Modern Sweden today. He was the first monarch to rule a unified Sweden. He ruled at the same time as Henry VIII of England, with whom he corresponded, and his rule was often as harsh as Henry's. Like Henry, Vasa joined the Protestant Reformation, not necessarily out of religious belief but because this would allow him, not the pope in Rome, to control religion in Sweden. More importantly, the money that the church, now the Church of Sweden, brought in would belong to him.

For the Finns, this meant yet another change in their religion because of Sweden.

Gustav I Vasa also founded the city of Helsingfors in 1550. Today, the world knows the city as Helsinki, which is the capital of Finland. Until Helsingfors/Helsinki became the capital of Finland in 1812, the most important city in Finland was Åbo, known as Turku today.

Sweden during and after Gustav I Vasa.

Under the Vasa kings and queens, Sweden grew into a great European power, and for a time in the late 17th century and early 18th century, it was a power broker in Europe. In 1630, Swedish King Gustavus II Adolphus, with a highly trained and professional Swedish/Finnish army, helped end the Thirty Years' War, which had decimated northern and central Europe. One of the more famous units in the Swedish army was Finnish, the Hakkapeliitta, a light cavalry unit that specialized in swift, surprising raids into and behind enemy lines. In 1940, while Finland was under assault from the Soviet Union, the Finnish government resurrected the spirit of the Hakkapeliitta to encourage its countrymen, many of whom specialized in cavalry and ski raids behind enemy lines, appearing from and disappearing into nowhere.

Hakkapeliitta stamp, 1940.
https://commons.wikimedia.org/wiki/File:Hakkapeliitta-1940.jpg

Finland was formally a part of Sweden at the time of Gustav Vasa. It would remain part of Sweden until 1809, when the two most powerful nations in Europe at the time, France and Russia, forced Sweden to relinquish control of Finland.

In the 17th and 18th centuries, most Finns thought of themselves not as Swedes but as part of the Swedish Empire, and to a very large degree, this benefited them. The population of Finland has always been small, especially considering the size of the territory, and in the late 17th and early 18th centuries, Russia was becoming more powerful and established varying levels of control in the Baltic region. The Russians also claimed parts of Karelia and areas around the new city of St. Petersburg. Sweden's army was a valuable hedge against future Russian moves against Finland, though, by 1809, Sweden's army was not capable of resisting both the French and Russians, who forced the cession of Finland without firing a shot.

Chapter 6 – Swedish Rule in Finland until 1809

The end of the Thirty Years' War, codified in the famous treaty known as the Peace of Westphalia (1639), ushered in a period of peace and relative stability in Sweden and Finland. From this time until the Great Northern War, which was fought between Russia and its allies (the Kingdom of Denmark and Norway and Saxony-Poland-Lithuania) and Sweden, great changes took place within Sweden (which included Finland). Many of these much-needed reforms set the groundwork for the modern Swedish and Finnish states.

One of Sweden's benefits was the formation of an informal trade association that involved the increasingly wealthy Protestant states of northern Europe (England, Denmark, many of the German states, and Holland). This alliance allowed for greater trade between Protestant states with a bit less competition from their Catholic neighbors to the south.

In 1634, a number of administrative reforms were enacted in Sweden that streamlined decision-making within the government and military, making them more responsive to the needs of the people and defense. A formal civil service was also created. The departments of the civil service were called colleges (called "ministries" in Finland, which had its own administrative structure under a Swedish governor-general, a nobleman appointed by the Swedish monarch). The colleges were responsible for things like agriculture, trade, defense,

and education, to name a few. From 1623 to 1637, Finland ha
governors-general.

By the time the third governor-general of Finland was appointed in
1637, most of the reforms that had been carried out in Sweden had
been established in Finland. However, Governor-General Count Per
Brahe the Younger is the best-known Finnish governor-general.

Brahe was governor-general of Finland twice, from 1637 to 1641
and 1648 to 1654. Administratively, Brahe presided during a period
of peace and stability within Finland and took credit for many of the
reforms that had been enacted before his arrival. However, he and his
administration did enact some important and beneficial reforms that
caused him to be remembered long after his death. People referred to
the years of his administration as the "time of the Count," and many
looked back on those years with some fondness.

In 1636, the Royal Mail of Sweden was founded. Within two years,
Brahe had built a post office in virtually all of the towns and cities (not
villages) of Finland. This made communication administration faster
and easier not only within Finland but also between Sweden and
Finland.

The Royal Academy of Åbo (now the Royal Academy of Turku) is
the oldest university in Finland. It was founded by the incredibly
interesting Queen Kristina (r. 1644–1654), who you can read about in
Captivating History's *History of Sweden.* Per Brahe supported this
idea wholeheartedly and is remembered as the man who oversaw its
construction and initial administration.

One of Brahe's greatest accomplishments was the building of new
towns in Finland. Brahe was very much like a king in Finland, and in
Sweden, the new monarch would traditionally take a tour on what was
called the "Royal Route," traveling to the interior of the country and
back. Brahe wasn't a king, but he did have almost absolute power in
Finland.

Per Brahe, c. 1650
https://commons.wikimedia.org/w/index.php?curid=28894119

When Per Brahe arrived as governor-general for the first time, he knew very little about the interior of the territory. His tour through Finland opened his eyes to the hard lives of the few Finns who lived there and to the economic possibilities of the country.

In the 17th century, the new economic idea was "mercantilism," the notion that an economy ran best when it was highly centralized and governed by strict rules that were designed to give it a favorable balance of trade. Mercantilism is often associated with the establishment of colonies that would benefit the mother country. In this case, the mother country was Sweden or, rather, the Swedish government, which had been on the road to becoming an absolute monarchy for some time.

Control was very important in the economic sphere. The Swedes set up an unusual system that, on the whole, benefited Swedes and Finns, at least in the cities, larger towns, and ports. A few population centers were declared "staple towns." Only staple towns had the right to trade internationally. The small number of these towns and the concentration of trade there meant it was easier for the government to tax and control trade coming into and leaving these centers. In

Finland, at least in Brahe's time, there were only three staple towns: Åbo, Helsinki, and Viborg (on the Karelian Isthmus near St. Petersburg). Greater wealth was concentrated in these three cities, which, in turn, drew more people to them, both from the Finnish interior and Sweden.

Towns that were not staple towns were only allowed to trade within Finland, and the government also oversaw this. So, those in the country towns and villages that wished to trade overseas had to go through merchants in the staple towns. They also had to pay a special tax. In turn, the staple town merchants would sell those goods overseas, and they were again taxed.

Though this system greatly benefited the Swedish Crown and Finland's governor-general, they were not the only ones. Brahe sponsored the founding of ten towns in Finland, which, generally speaking, improved the lives of many Finns. These towns, which were located in the interior of the country and on the relatively undeveloped southeastern coast, brought in Finns, Swedes, and foreigners, mostly wealthy Germans and Danes. Though Sweden and the towns of western Finland traded with Russia, most of their overseas business was done with western and central Europe. The new towns in the southeast mainly did business with the Baltic states and Russia.

Slowly, the country grew more prosperous, though Finland and most Finns were not nearly as wealthy as Sweden and most Swedes. By 1700, Finland, while still a relative "backwater" compared to Sweden, Denmark, and even poorer Norway, was much more prosperous than anyone could have expected in 1639 when Brahe began his first term as governor-general.

Trade Goods

Until the early 17th century, only about 5 percent of the Finnish population engaged in something other than fishing, farming, and hunting. Most surplus grain was paid as tax. In the early 17th century, Europe experienced the greatest economic boom it had ever known. The colonial empires of England, Holland, Spain, and Portugal supplied much of Europe with goods from Asia, Africa, and the Middle East. Spain and Portugal had begun their slow decline in the early 17th century and were distant Catholic powers that Sweden had little to do with. However, England and Holland were growing richer by the day, and Swedish economic ties with both countries went back centuries. In the later 17th and early 18th centuries, economic ties between Sweden and France, continental Europe's richest and most powerful nation at the time, also increased.

Holland and England built more ships as overseas trade increased in the 17th and 18th centuries. They built thousands of ships. One result of such a massive shipbuilding program was the almost complete deforestation of both countries. Before the use of steel to build ships, the nations of Europe that had the most forested lands had an economic boom. And no territory in Europe was more forested than Sweden, Finland, and Norway.

In Norway and Sweden, which were more technologically advanced compared to Finland and whose trees were generally more suited to shipbuilding and other finished products, lumber mills cut down trees and created lumber to specification.

Much of Finland was pine forests. Pine trees are the source of pitch and tar, both necessary in building ships. In the mid-17th century, tar (the more useful and effective of the two products) made up about 2 percent of Finland's exports. Before the end of the century, tar made up nearly 10 percent. Of that 10 percent, about 75 percent of Finland's tar production came from the eastern part of the country, which had traditionally been the poorer region. The Swedes did not have a monopoly on tar production and trade, but they dominated it and were able to control prices through the sheer volume of tar they produced and shipped. Think of the Swedes as the 17th-century version of OPEC (Organization of the Petroleum Exporting Countries), except they dealt in tar rather than petroleum.

Another benefit of the vast Swedish and Finnish forests was that the trees could be turned into charcoal, which was needed for iron- and steel-smelting. In an age before the widespread use of coal, timber was needed to make iron. The Dutch and especially the English had iron deposits, but they lacked the wood to make charcoal. This was where the Swedes came in. Though there were only about thirty ironworks in Finland, there were over three hundred in Sweden. Finished copper production also relied on wood/charcoal, and both Sweden and Finland had plenty of both. Copper and iron production in the Swedish Empire rose until the early 18th century, and even then, copper production comprised about 25 percent of Sweden's exports.

Religion

Absolute monarchies reached their greatest heights in Europe during the 17th and 18th centuries. Even in England, where the monarch's power was restrained by Parliament, the ruler held tremendous power. This was the same (albeit to an even greater extent) in mainland Europe, with the exception of Holland, which had become, at least to a degree, a republic after it won its independence from Spain in 1581.

In the Catholic kingdoms, monarchs often vied with the church for a greater share of power. In France under Louis XIV (considered the "ultimate" absolute monarch), the state, for the most part, managed to control the church's power to a large degree. In Spain, from the early 17th century onward, both the church and nobility worked incessantly to weaken or control the monarch's power, meeting much success.

In central Europe, meaning the German states and what would later become Czechoslovakia, the population was split between Protestants and Catholics, making absolute power hard to come by. The only significant German absolute monarchy was in the northeastern kingdom of Prussia, where almost the entire population was Protestant Lutheran.

In Denmark and Sweden (until relatively recently, Norway was always the "poor cousin" of the Scandinavian countries and was alternately part of Denmark and Sweden at times), the Protestant Lutheran Church was the only religion. Though there were Catholics in both countries, they were persecuted and punished economically to a large degree. This was much more prevalent in Sweden than in Denmark.

Protestantism had begun to split into a number of different sects by the late 17th century, but the teachings of Martin Luther were still the foundation for them. And though the Protestant kings and nobles fought exceedingly bloody wars for their right to choose their religion, this freedom of worship did not trickle down to the populace. In Sweden and Finland, a harsh Lutheran fundamentalism took hold. Religious toleration did not become law in Sweden until 1781, and even then, Catholics experienced widespread discrimination.

This book is meant to be an introduction to Finnish history, and unfortunately, an in-depth study of religious fundamentalism in

Scandinavia is outside its scope. But suffice it to say, like most fundamentalist sects, those in Sweden and Finland established requirements for church attendance, manner of living, types of speech, and books the population were allowed to read and those they were not. The vast majority of printed works in Scandinavia and Finland at this time were religious. Reading for enjoyment or enlightenment outside of religious readings was either proscribed or severely frowned upon.

This does not mean that the Swedes established something like a modern police surveillance state. They didn't have to; peer pressure and beliefs did much of the policing for them. In virtually all Protestant churches at the time, the "fire and brimstone" sermon took root. Fear of hell kept many people in line at a time when being different or an outsider was dangerous. Much of the population was ignorant, meaning they weren't properly educated.

What education the people had came from the Lutheran Church. Since the Protestants believed the Bible was the literal word of God, they believed each person should have access to it (even if they were told how to interpret it by the clergy). Thus, literacy in the Nordic countries was (and still is) among the highest in the world.

What's more, religion was a unifying element in Swedish and Finnish societies. Most of the religious education was done in Swedish, and during the 17th and 18th centuries, this was done without much resentment on the part of the Finns. The period saw a growth in the wealth of most people, and Finnish was not prohibited. Most Finns were loyal to the Swedish Crown to some degree or other, and since much of the southwest was populated by Swedes, there was some degree of intermarriage. Ethnic conflicts between Swedes and Finns were kept at a minimum.

Chapter 7 – Swedish Decline

For much of the 17th century, Sweden was one of the great European powers. It could even be said that it was a world power. From 1638 to 1655, the Swedes even had an overseas colony called New Sweden. You might know it as Delaware. The Swedes also had a relatively unbroken series of kings who were skilled soldiers, and they had one of the first professional standing (full-time) armies in the world.

In 1658, the Swedes pushed the Danish king and most of the Danish people out of mainland Sweden once and for all. By this point, they had fought many of the armies of Europe and, in most cases, won, oftentimes with fewer men.

By 1721, Sweden's place as a European power was done. In 1809, its place as a regional power was unsteady. The defeats that Sweden sustained on the battlefield and at the negotiating table meant that the Finns were susceptible to growing foreign influence and control, with most of that influence, especially from the late 18th century onward, coming from Russia.

From 1611 to 1718, the Swedes had five monarchs: Gustavus II Adolphus (the only Swedish king called "the Great"), the controversial but brilliant Kristina I, Charles (Karl) X Gustav, Charles XI, and Charles XII. Though Kristina was not a field general, she understood strategy well and wisely appointed her generals and advisers. There is a general consensus that all of the Swedish kings of this period were gifted military leaders, though the last, Charles XII, overestimated his ability and underestimated his enemy. By the end of his reign, Sweden had become a second-rate power.

The Northern Wars

Sweden took part in many conflicts during its history, but the three we are going to examine were called the Northern Wars. There is some confusion about the name of these wars, but for our purposes, the First Northern War took place from 1558 to 1583. It was between Sweden and its allies (Denmark, Poland, and Lithuania) on one side and Russia. The war ended in a Swedish victory, with Sweden making some territorial gains. The Second Northern War (also known as the Livonian War, lasting from 1655 to 1660) was fought against Poland. The Second Northern War was fought over the succession to the Swedish throne. There had been kings of Sweden who were also Polish, and this conflict put an end to Polish claims on the Swedish crown.

The Third Northern War is also known as the Great Northern War. It lasted from 1700 to 1721 and was fought between Sweden and Russia (the latter of which was joined by Saxony, the union of Poland and Lithuania, and Denmark-Norway). The Swedes were joined by a number of allies, but most of them were smaller states, with the exception of the Ottoman Empire, which was in decline at the time. The British and Dutch also allied with Sweden, but they were too far away to make any real significant impact on the conflict.

At first, the Great Northern War seemed as if it was going to end like the other Northern Wars had, with a Swedish victory. Over and over, the professional armies of Sweden, which consisted of large numbers of Finns, were greatly outnumbered but won victory after victory in both the west and east.

In 1709, Charles XII drove deep into Russia and Ukraine. At Poltava in present-day Ukraine, Charles made some uncharacteristic mistakes. He ignored intelligence about Russian numbers and fortifications and did not give clear commands to his generals. Poltava was a disaster for the Swedes and allowed the Russian tsar, Peter I (known as Peter the Great), to proclaim a Russian Empire, which included the Baltic states, Ukraine, and parts of Poland.

Charles's return to Sweden took years, and his journeys took him as far away as modern Turkey. When he returned to Sweden in 1713, he found Sweden under siege by its enemies, some of whom had once been his allies, like Great Britain. During the last phase of the war, Sweden lost all of its overseas territories, including parts of northern Norway that had been nominally Swedish for centuries.

Though Charles and his generals won a number of victories against great odds in Europe and Norway, Charles was killed in Norway while besieging the town of Fredrikshald. He was shot clean through the head while inspecting Swedish trenches. With Charles's death, the Great Northern War ended, and his daughter, Ulrika, became queen of Sweden. One of the few territories the Swedes kept was Finland, but Swedish control of Finland would end in just a few decades.

Chapter 8 – Russian Crown Colony

At the end of the Great Northern War, Russia had gained Swedish/Finnish territory, the land bridge north of St. Petersburg and a bit beyond, through the Treaty of Nystad. In the 1740s, internal strife in Sweden led to increased Russian influence in Finland and Sweden. A period of struggle ensued among the Swedes, and another war (1741-1742) was waged with Russia over control of Finland, especially its southern ports. In the Treaty of Åbo (1743), the Russians were given more territories.

The green indicates areas given to Russia in 1721 and the yellow in 1743. Remember this map, for this would essentially be the final settlement of the Finnish border after the Winter War with the USSR in 1940.

By Janneman, CC BY 3.0 <https://creativecommons.org/licenses/by/3.0>, via Wikimedia Commons; https://commons.wikimedia.org/w/index.php?curid=757077

In 1789, the French Revolution began. The effects of the French Revolution on Finland were indirect but profound. The revolution began as a rebellion against the rule of the absolute monarchy of Louis XVI and the Ancien Régime, the "ancient" ruling class of kings and aristocrats.

Outside France, the French Revolution greatly affected the many states of what would become Germany in 1871. There were dozens of German states, which included principalities, duchies, kingdoms, and independent cities. Some were extremely small, while others, especially Bavaria and Prussia, were large. Most were controlled or heavily influenced by other nations or more powerful German states, but Austria, France, and Denmark either directly or indirectly controlled or influenced many.

In France, the rebellion against Louis XVI quickly spiraled into a violent and radical revolution that removed the king and queen (and their heads), the privileges of the nobility, and much of the Catholic Church's power. Soon, France was at war with much of Europe, whose monarchs and ruling classes feared the spread of revolutionary ideas in their territories.

The victories of the French forces, both the revolutionaries and the man who succeeded them, Napoleon Bonaparte, spread the ideas of the French Revolution, especially the ideas that emphasized democratic ideals and self-determination. In France, self-determination (a later historical term from WWI but which is appropriate here) meant the people's freedom to determine their own form of government. This applied to almost all of Europe but was more a reference to the German states being free from foreign occupation and control.

Of course, Napoleon's rule outside of France was just as oppressive as within France, but the spread of the biggest revolutionary idea, nationalism, could not be contained. In Sweden, where the monarchy's power slowly declined in the later 18th and early 19th centuries, many called for a more representative government.

In the 1780s, Swedish society was increasingly divided, at least at the top. Two factions, one supported by France and the other influenced by Russia, fought for control of the country. In 1786, the king, Gustav III, came out on top and reestablished an absolute monarchy similar to what had existed before. Like the French, the

Swedish people and nobility were growing tired of the king's oppressive rule. And to add to an already volatile situation, Gustav, without seeking the approval of Parliament, which violated his own constitution, declared war on Russia in 1788. This caused a mutiny among the liberal officers in the army, and Gustav was put down ruthlessly. The war with Russia provided Sweden with its greatest naval victory in history, but it did not settle anything. The Treaty of Värälä, which ended the war, only reinforced the borders that the countries had before the war began.

However, in March 1792, things changed within Sweden. A plot by nobles, who wished to diminish the power of the king, succeeded. Gustav III was assassinated, though it took him thirteen days to die of his wounds. Some of the plotters had been supported by France.

The new king, Gustavus IV Adolf, would eventually join one of the many coalitions against Napoleon, but neither he nor the Swedish army bore much resemblance to the powerful Swedish forces of the 17th and early 18th centuries.

One of Napoleon's admirers, the young tsar of Russia, Alexander I, did not join sides in the Napoleonic Wars. A complicated series of events began when Alexander I and Napoleon met at Tilsit (today known as Sovetsk in the Russian territory of Kaliningrad on the Baltic Sea). As a result of being defeated by Napoleon, Sweden was forced to cede Finland to Russia per the agreement made between the Russian tsar and the French emperor.

In Sweden, the military defeat and humiliating loss of Finland after centuries of Swedish rule resulted in the overthrow of Gustavus IV Adolf by disenchanted nobles and the businessmen of the country (who were often one and the same). In his place, the Swedes, through a truly strange series of events too long to describe here, offered the crown to one of Napoleon's field marshals, Jean Bernadotte, who accepted and became Charles (Karl) XIV Johann of Sweden, the founder of the present-day Swedish royal family.

On the face of it, one would think that the new Swedish king would be nothing but a tool of Napoleon's, but when he accepted the Swedes' invitation and sought Napoleon's blessing, he told the French emperor that his new responsibility was to his new kingdom, not his old emperor. And he meant it. Charles XIV established a policy of neutrality, which guided Swedish foreign policy from 1810 until 2022 when, in the face of Russian aggression in Ukraine, Sweden (and Finland) applied to join NATO.

Finnish Nationalism

French revolutionary ideas included nationalism and self-determination. Though the latter term originated at the end of WWI, it works as an explanation of what began to happen in Finland, especially among the Finnish elite, including university professors, writers, poets, and higher-level bureaucrats.

It would take a few decades for the feeling that Finns should govern themselves to become a popular cause among the general population. However, the feeling grew until the last quarter or so of the 19th century when the Fennoman movement began to have a real impact, not just politically but also among the people themselves.

For centuries, Finland had been part of Sweden. Perhaps if Swedish rule had continued, the Finnish nationalist feeling would have gained traction in the late 19th century, but we do know that this feeling increased in popularity under Russian rule, especially as the 19th century headed toward the 20th century.

Russian Rule, Pt. I

In 1721, Russia took control of the Karelian Isthmus and the area around Lake Ladoga. In 1743, the Russians gained more territories and forced the Swedes to agree that Sweden would not enter into any foreign alliances without Russian approval. The latter stipulation would not last long, but in 1810, the Swedes decided on the policy of neutrality, which lasted until 2022.

In the 18th century, Russian rule in the parts of Finland it controlled was, relative to what came later, somewhat benign. Part of this was due to the nature of Russian expansionism and government. Even before the time of Peter the Great, Russia had been expanding its territory, but under Peter and his successors, this expansion increased.

Given the size of the territory, the state of communications between the 17th and late 19th centuries, and the nature of Russian absolutism, the governance of new territories happened rather haphazardly. One of the benefits of this was that, especially in Finland, the bureaucracy was left relatively unchanged. Compared to the wild and sparsely populated areas of the east and south that Russia colonized during this period, the central Finnish administrative state was advanced.

The Finns in this territory had been "Swedish" for so long and knew that the geopolitical situation meant they were left on their own. Those living near the borders of Russia, for the most part, accommodated themselves to Russian rule. For Russia, a peaceful, relatively prosperous population on their border meant more income from taxes and that thousands of Russian troops, who were needed elsewhere, did not have to be posted in Finland.

To the surprise of many, the Russians did not force Eastern Orthodoxy on the Finns and kept Swedish laws in effect. Poor landless Finns were not forced into serfdom, as had been the case in Russia for centuries. During Swedish rule, peasants had often risen up to protect their rights to certain lands and when the rule of the nobility became too oppressive. These rebellions, especially the Cudgel War of 1596–1597, were put down violently, but peasant uprisings were always at the forefront of the minds of rulers who were debating new policies. The international culture and thriving economy of the largest Finnish city on the isthmus, Vyborg (in Finnish, Viipuri), also benefited the Russians and promoted the continuance of a benign rule.

Russian Rule, Pt. II

In 1809, the Swedish defeat and the negotiations between France and Russia resulted in all of Finland being given to Russia in the Treaty of Fredrikshamn. Finland was designated a grand duchy under the control of the Russian tsar, who functioned as the grand duke of Finland. The tsar, in turn, appointed a governor who was responsible only to the monarch. At times, the Finns enjoyed a measure of self-rule that other parts of the Russian Empire could only dream of. For instance, Finns were not required to serve in the Imperial Russian Army, though quite a few did, especially among the upper classes.

Mannerheim, the man who would be declared the "greatest Finn of all time" in 2008, was a Swedish Finn whose family had roots in Germany and who spoke Swedish, German, and Russian better than he spoke Finnish. He was one of these upper-class officers and was present at the crowning of the last Russian tsar, Nicholas II, in 1896. (Nicholas took the throne in 1894.) Similar to the Swedish monarchy, the Finns were represented by a one-house parliament called the Diet from 1809 to 1906 and Parliament from 1906 to 1917. There, matters pertaining to Finland were debated, and laws were passed as long as they did not run counter to Russian policy. Mannerheim's great-grandfather was a senator and one of the very first to hold the important office of vice chairman of the Economic Division, which, despite its name, was very much akin to that of the modern Finnish prime minister. Mannerheim's grandfather was governor of the Vyborg principality for a time as well.

All Russian governors-general of Finland were members of the nobility. Most of them held political office in Russia as well. Occasionally, some of them decided to suppress "Finnish-ness" and promote more direct Russian rule. They promoted Russian culture over Finnish, including the Orthodox religion. This likely happened out of personal political reasons, a sense of Russian superiority, or because they were unfamiliar with the spirit of Finnish independence and wished the Finns to be "Russified" like many other minorities in Russia had been.

This first happened in 1824 when Russian Count Arseny Zakrevsky was appointed governor-general of Finland. Zakrevsky also held the powerful position of minister of the interior of Russia; in other words, he was the head of Russia's police and secret police, the Okhrana, among other things.

When Zakrevsky took office, he immediately began to bypass both the Finnish Diet and the Finnish secretary of state, who presented Finnish laws to the tsar for approval. Zakrevsky took that right and the influence that went with it. And like many other high-ranking Russian nobles, Zakrevsky angled for an influential position when Alexander I died in December 1825. Zakrevsky and others believed that the next tsar would be Constantine, Alexander's younger brother. In order to win favor with the new "tsar to be," Zakrevsky promoted a law that required the Finns to swear an oath of absolute loyalty to the tsar, something they were not inclined to do.

Unfortunately for Zakrevsky, Constantine lost a power struggle with his younger brother, Nicholas, who became Nicholas I, "Tsar of all the Russias," just before the New Year, 1826. Upon taking the throne, Nicholas promised the Finns that their traditional rights would be respected. Zakrevsky lost the battle but remained governor-general until 1831.

In many ways, Russian policy in Finland was unique among the other territories Russia controlled, at least in the first part of the 19th century. In many areas, particularly in the Russian-controlled parts of Poland (Austria and Prussia controlled the other two-thirds) and Ukraine, violent uprisings for independence took place, which were put down with great violence. In Ukraine especially, Russian policy included the forced use of the Russian language and direct and harsh rule by Russian governors and generals.

This did not take place in Finland, at least not directly. Zakrevsky and others within the Russian government and nobility favored a policy that became known as gradual Russification. The Russian language would be encouraged in business, and since Finland's trade involved Russia to one degree or another, many Finnish nobles, merchants, and businessmen began to learn Russian to make their way up the Finnish and Russian economic and social ladders. For instance, Mannerheim's Russian was much better than his Finnish for most of his life.

The Fennoman Movement

Despite the fact that speaking Russian was encouraged, especially among upper-class Finns, Swedish was still the language of most business transactions within Finland (especially in the south), of government, and of literature. Some Russians, both within Russia and in Finland itself, actually encouraged the use of Finnish but not necessarily out of liberal ideals. The thinking behind this was that if Russians encouraged the use of Finnish, at least among Finns, it would separate Finnish culture and the Finns themselves from Sweden, which was still a regional power.

In 1863, Finnish was recognized as the official language of the country, with Swedish being the other official language. However, about 15 percent of the country and almost all of the ruling upper class only spoke Swedish or used it as their preferred language. This is significant. If you recall, one of the main reasons that Protestantism spread throughout Europe was because of the translations of the Bible from Latin into national languages. Until that time, Christians were dependent on the Catholic clergy to educate them on religious matters.

In the same way, people who only spoke Finnish were at a disadvantage in their own country. Since most of the larger businesses used Swedish, only those who could speak that language could participate. The same held true for governmental matters and the press. Though most Finns were far from illiterate, until the second half of the 19th century, they had to rely on the goodwill of others for knowledge of what was happening in their country and the world.

For much of its history, Finland had been part of a larger whole. Luckily, its size, geography, climate, circumstances, and the occasional violent uprising kept it from suffering from the fate of so many other colonies around the world. The Finns didn't deal with the complete loss of independence, the destruction of their culture, or the assimilation of their people.

The fear of assimilation and the rise in nationalism in the 19th century caused a number of Finns, mostly from the educated and upper class (who were, most of the time, one and the same) and whose primary language was Swedish, to promote Finnish as a way of protecting Finnish culture and creating a nationalist feeling based on shared history, values, and culture.

The Fennoman movement (sometimes known as Fennomania in Sweden and Finland—and no, in this instance, "mania" does not mean a focused type of insanity; it loosely translates as "Finnishness") was a literary movement that championed Finnish in the publication of classic literature, newspapers, and newly written works, including academic works.

In the early 19th century, changes in government censorship in much of western and central Europe, education policy, and printing technology meant that more people were reading than ever before. In Germany, one of the most literate countries in the world, reading actually became a "fad" of sorts. New scientific discoveries, new and brilliant literature written in German (rather than Latin, for instance), and much else made the discussion of books and ideas extremely popular in Germany. The "reading rage," or *Lesewut*, spread to Sweden and then to Finland by the early 1830s.

This gave rise to the Fennoman movement, which became the primary movement of Finnish nationalism until Finland won its independence shortly after WWI. The most popular example of Finnish-language literature was the publication of the *Kalevala* in 1835.

You have already learned about Elias Lönnrot and the *Kalevala*, but the importance of the *Kalevala*'s publication went beyond just the use of the Finnish language in a major literary work. The *Kalevala* promoted a sense of exclusively Finnish history and culture that had not existed before.

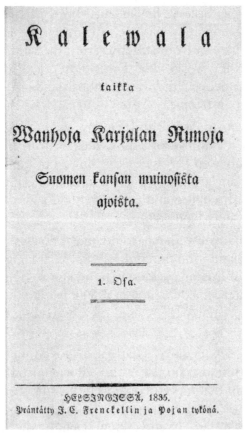

A first edition of the *Kalevala*, 1835.
https://commons.wikimedia.org/wiki/File:Kalevala1.jpg

Two other leading figures from the early Fennoman period were J. V. Snellman and J. L. Runeberg. Snellman was a politician, journalist, and writer, and Runeberg was a priest who also published popular books and tracts on Finnish culture and history. Ironically, both men wrote exclusively in Swedish.

The Fennoman movement was opposed by a loose-knit group of writers, politicians, and professors known as the Svecomans, who promoted the continued use and spread of Swedish rather than

Finnish. Others opposed to the Fennoman movement and its beliefs, which became more political and less cultural as the 19th century went on, were the leaders of the church in Finland, most of whom were either Swedes or Swedish-speaking Finns, and the Russian authorities, who were always alert to the possibility of rebellion within their empire.

The struggle to get Finnish recognized as one of the territory's official languages ended in 1863. However, to get to that point, the Finnish and the Fennomans had to endure some hard times. By the late 1840s, Tsar Nicholas I had become more and more conservative and autocratic, allowing himself to be convinced, mostly by conservative clerics in Finland, to outlaw the use of Finnish in all written works that were not religious in nature. Of course, that only encouraged the Fennomans (who, as you learned above, included a number of Swedish-speaking Finns, many of whom changed their names to more "Finnish-sounding" ones). It also caused more Finns to become resentful of foreign rule and cultural dominance.

Russian Rule, Pt. III

Just because Russian rule in Finland was somewhat more benign compared to some of the other territories of the Russian Empire does not mean that the Finns liked it. Some at the very top made the best of a bad situation and attempted to climb the Russian social ladder in St. Peterburg, which, after all, was only a few miles from Finland. Rich merchants and traders had a distinct advantage over their Swedish counterparts since most Swedes dealing with Russians used Finnish middlemen or landed in Finnish ports. The Finns also sold some Western goods in Russia, but Finnish furs, timber, and tar (at least until the end of the age of wooden sailing ships) were in high demand for most of the Russian rule.

As you just discovered, many upper-class and aristocratic Finns were part of the Fennoman movement, which gave birth to the idea of an independent Finnish nation and the importance of the Finnish language.

Finns in the lower-middle and lower agricultural class also grew bitter about the increasingly autocratic Russian regime in the last part of the 19th century. Not all were happy with Russian rule, and the people grew increasingly unhappy by the turn of the century. Unfortunately, though Finns in the lower classes had representation in the Finnish Parliament, you can likely guess they had no real power and lacked leaders who had the charisma, influence, and desire to move Finland toward independence.

In 2022, the Russo-Ukrainian War began. One of Vladimir Putin's stated goals was that Russia was concerned that NATO would spread into Ukraine. He also made remarks that Russia was against NATO expansion retroactively and made demands that NATO roll itself back to its pre-1991 borders in western Europe. "NATO expansion" was one of the ways Putin attempted to "sell" the invasion of Ukraine to the Russian people. As you may know, his invasion of Ukraine alarmed Europe, specifically Finland and Sweden, two nations that had an official policy of neutrality for decades and centuries, respectively. As a result of Putin's Ukrainian invasion, both Finland and Sweden applied for NATO membership. His plan had the exact opposite effect from what he intended.

In the same way, the Russians of the late 19th century wished to make Finland a more integrated part of the Russian Empire. The man who would carry out this more radical and sudden plan of the "Russification" of Finland was Nikolai Bobrikov, who was appointed governor-general of Finland and commander of the Finnish Military District in 1898.

Bobrikov.
https://commons.wikimedia.org/w/index.php?curid=1651153

Bobrikov was appointed by Tsar Nicholas II, who had taken the Russian throne in 1894. Despite the hopes of some more liberal-minded Russians, Nicholas proved himself to be the autocrat his father was and became influenced by hardline conservatives in the royal family, including his wife and the Russian Orthodox Church. The idea that Finland had a great degree of autonomy and its own parliament rankled Nicholas and many of the most powerful men in the Russian aristocracy. They felt that territories controlled by Russia should speak Russian, act Russian (by adopting Russian customs, traditions, modes of dress, and, most importantly, governance), and worship like Russians.

Though many of the Finnish elite, especially in the east of the country and in the military, did speak Russian, at least to a degree, most Finns did not want to speak Russian and made little attempt to learn how. They certainly didn't want to "act Russian" or change their religion. In 1899, the most famous Finnish composer Jean Sibelius wrote his haunting and majestic piece, *Finlandia*, in reaction to increasing Russian intrusion on Finnish life. Through music, the piece tells the story of Finnish history and is still the most famous piece of music ever written by a Finn.

Bobrikov helped ensure the Finns would resent Russian rule and be less likely to accept anything Russian, from the language to its church.

Once Bobrikov took office, he almost immediately put his plan into action for the Russification of Finland. His program included the adoption of Russian as the official language of Finland, limiting the power of the Finnish secretary of state (who represented Finland at the tsar's court), and fully integrating the Finnish armed forces into the Imperial Russian Army. This meant Finns would not be in all-Finnish units but spread among Russian forces throughout the empire. They would be far from home and far from creating any disturbances in their homeland.

In this painting, *Hyökkäys* (known as *The Attack* in English), the double-headed Russian eagle is attacking Finland, who is trying to save her laws and independence. It was painted in 1899 by Edvard Isto.
https://commons.wikimedia.org/wiki/File:Suomineito.jpg

A year after taking office, it was clear that Bobrikov had the full support of Nicholas II. In 1899, the tsar signed a decree that gave him the right to overturn any legislation passed in Finland. For the most part, the Finns had the right to make decisions within their own borders for centuries, including their time under Russian rule. In response, 500,000 Finns (about 25 percent of the population) signed a petition asking Nicholas to rescind his decree. By all accounts, Nicholas never even looked at the petition when it arrived at his palace. He should have, though, as the sheer number of signatures might have changed his mind about his rule in Finland.

In 1900, Russian was made the official language of all government business, and Russian language instruction was increased in Finnish schools. Finnish officials in certain government offices, particularly offices governing the country's many lighthouses and railroads, were replaced by Russians. Russian stamps replaced Finnish ones, which simply reminded the Finns every day of the increasing Russian control over their country. Throughout Finland, especially in the cities, Russian security officials watched to see who opposed Bobrikov's policies. As you can likely imagine, many vocal opponents of these policies were arrested. Many were tortured, which was a common punishment for those accused of sedition within Russia itself.

In 1902, the first draft of Finns for the integrated Imperial Russian Army took place. Less than half of those who were called showed up. Three years later, the Russians called off the Finnish draft, saying the Finns were "unreliable," which actually meant that the tsar was afraid of a Finnish war of independence.

The Finns call the period of time under Bobrikov until the end of World War I *Sortovuodet* (the "Years of Oppression"). Unfortunately for Bobrikov, his plan backfired. A group of Finnish nobles began a debate on whether Bobrikov should be assassinated or not. One of these men, an ethnic Swedish Finn named Eugen Schauman (who, incidentally, was born in Kharkiv, Ukraine), shot Bobrikov three times on June 16th, 1904. Bobrikov died the next day. Schauman knew that an extended period of torture would follow, so he killed himself after shooting the governor-general. Though he is remembered less today than in the period immediately after the assassination and Finland's independence in 1917, Schauman is still considered a national hero in Finland.

After the death of Bobrikov, Russia suspended some of its measures against Finland. This was not a result of the assassination but rather the Russian fear of even wider unrest in Finland. Russia itself was facing discontent, with the people growing tired of the autocratic system of the tsars and upset over the humiliating defeat of Russia at the hands of the Japanese in the Russo-Japanese War of 1905. Unrest (including the infamous Bloody Sunday in January 1905, in which hundreds, if not thousands, of peaceful demonstrators were gunned down in St. Petersburg) spread throughout Russia and threatened Tsar Nicholas II's rule. One of the byproducts of the Russo-Japanese War was the sale of weapons by the Japanese to the Finns, which were later used against the Russians and in the Finnish Civil War of 1918, which followed World War One.

However, in 1908, the second period of the *Sortovuodet* began. The measures enacted in this period went further than what even Bobrikov had pushed for. In 1910, a law was decreed in Russia that replaced all Finnish parliamentarians with Finnish officers of the Imperial Russian Army. Russia imposed a heavy tax on Finns for not renewing conscription. Also, in 1910, all power of the Finnish Parliament was given to the Russian Duma (a newly formed representative body that, until the latter stages of WWI, did the tsar's bidding). In 1912, the Law of Equality was passed, which forced all Finnish civil and governmental positions to open to Russians. During WWI, these measures were suspended for fear of an untimely Finnish revolt but were fully intended to be restored when the Russians won the Great War.

Finns of the Royal Prussian 27th Jäger Battalion in Latvia, also a Russian possession before the war, summer of 1917.

https://commons.wikimedia.org/wiki/File:Jaakaripataljooa_libaussa.jpg

By the time WWI began in August 1914, many Finns had become determined to fight for their independence after the war was over. Thousands of Finns traveled to Germany and fought as Finnish Jägers ("hunters" or light infantry) on the Eastern Front against the Russians during the war. In 1918, the survivors of these formations returned to Finland to begin what they believed would be a fight against Russia. Additionally, many German soldiers traveled to Finland to join their Finnish comrades. The German military sold much equipment to the Finns to fight Russian influence, prevent weapons from falling into Allied hands, and make money. Russia's policy had clearly backfired.

Chapter 9 – WWI, Civil War, and Independence

Finland's role in World War One was relatively small. Because the conscription laws had been suspended before the start of WWI and because Russia did not want to provoke a Finnish uprising on its northern flank, only a small number of Finns (under one thousand) served alongside the Russian forces in the war. Many of these men were from the Swedish-speaking elite, including Mannerheim, who you will learn more about shortly. More Finns went to fight for Germany than for Russia. The Finns who fought were not only aristocratic officers but also a larger percentage of soldiers and non-commissioned officers and sergeants. These men provided critical leadership and training to the Finnish "Whites," the anti-communist, conservative forces of the Finnish Civil War, which would follow World War One.

By 1917, Russia's grand ideas of victory against Germany and Austria-Hungary were in shambles. Its troops were hungry and did not have enough supplies of weapons and clothing. Many of the officers (many of whom were of the hated aristocracy) seemed to care more about personal glory than the lives of their men. Sounds rather familiar.

Additionally, a variety of socialist movements, including the Bolsheviks, who were led by Vladimir Lenin, were on the verge of a revolution in the major cities of Russia, particularly St. Petersburg, the capital. In 1917, Lenin was living in exile in Switzerland when food riots and protests broke out in Russia. Additionally, Russian troops at the front either simply left the fighting and started to head home or mutinied against their officers and formed leftist revolutionary units instead. These units were more concerned with fighting the tsarist system than the Germans and formed the core of what would become the Red Army. Of course, Lenin played a significant role in all of this.

In April 1917, Lenin found himself an unexpected ally: the German Empire. The Germans agreed to escort Lenin safely and secretly to the Russian border via Sweden and Finland and provide money for his planned revolution. In return, Lenin promised that should he become the new leader of Russia, he would immediately make peace with Germany along the front lines that currently existed, which meant that Germany would rule Ukraine and a large portion of Russia south of St. Petersburg and west of Moscow.

Surprisingly, both parties kept their word, and after the success of the Bolshevik Revolution, the new Union of Soviet Socialist Republics (USSR) made peace with Germany and confirmed its territorial gains, which Lenin likely knew Germany would lose, either through defeat by the Allies or its eventual defeat by a resurgent Russia.

Independence

One of the first things that Lenin did when he came to power surprised almost everyone, including some in Lenin's inner circle, particularly Joseph Stalin. On January 4th, 1918, Lenin recognized Finland as an independent country. Even in the time before the arrival of the Swedes in the Early Middle Ages, the Finns did not have a country but rather a number of tribal kingdoms that often fought one another.

Lenin recognized Finland's independence. He did not "grant" it. Granting something was only kings and tsars did. Moreover, with Russia's mounting losses in the war, Tsar Nicholas's preoccupation with it, and internal Russian dissent, the Finns had begun to take gradual control of their own affairs. By January 1918, they had control of their country in all but name.

The Soviet document that recognized Finnish independence signed by Lenin, Stalin, Trotsky, and others

Some American historians called the US Civil War the "Second American Revolution" or the "American Revolution 2.0" since many issues, from slavery to federal powers and state rights, had not been adequately settled with the defeat of Britain in 1781. Similarly, Finns (and this word now includes all the people living in Finland: Finns, Swedes, and the Sami, the native people of the north) had never had the opportunity to truly debate the form of government they would create if they gained independence.

In the last two decades of the 19th century and the early decades of the 20th, a number of different groups emerged in Finland, all with varying and sometimes widely diverging opinions of what Finland should look like as an independent nation. Even the Fennoman movement, which had become less of a cultural movement and more of a political one by the 20th century, had split into factions, with some advocating a limited Finnish monarchy along the lines of Sweden or Britain and others calling for an American- or French-style representative government. Still, others called for some form of socialism, including Soviet-style communism.

The Finnish Civil War

The early 20th century was a time of great political change and upheaval. Even the most stable countries were rocked by large and sometimes violent labor strikes and the occasional act of political terrorism. For most of Finland's history, the Finns had been able to avoid civil violence. You have just finished learning about the reasons for this: foreign control by Sweden and Russia. Independence was not necessarily a surprise, given the world situation and US President Woodrow Wilson's call for self-determination of the people. If there were ever a group of people that wanted that self-determination, it was the Finns.

Finland was very lucky in a way, for most believe that if Lenin had refused the Finnish move toward independence, war would have ensued between Finland and the Soviet Union. This might have been a war the Soviets could not win, especially since hundreds of thousands of Red Army soldiers were busy fighting hundreds of thousands of White Army troops (those who wished to reinstate the Russian royal family or establish a non-communist military dictatorship). War against Finland might have resulted in a White victory and the end of the Soviet Union.

In Helsinki today, there is a park named after Vladimir Lenin. Many foreigners wonder why the Finns would name this park after Lenin. For a time, there was even a statue of Lenin. As any Finn will tell you, this park is less a memorial to Lenin than it is a reminder of Finnish stubbornness because, after Lenin, many Russians wanted Finland back. Truth be told, so did Lenin, and the Bolsheviks had supported Finnish communists to a degree even before independence. When the Finnish Civil War began, that assistance (mostly in the form of troops and advisers, along with some weapons) continued.

This book is a general history of Finland and, by necessity, covers most, but not all, of the main events that shaped the country politically, militarily, and globally, with a bit of economics thrown in. Unfortunately, that means much of the fascinating cultural history of Finland and some of the country's internal political and economic events have to be overlooked.

As the 20th century approached and ideas about representative democracy and various kinds of socialism spread, the middle and lower classes of Finland began to play a more significant role in society and politics.

Having been the subjects of two monarchies, most Finns had never truly had a voice in the country, at least not one that could be heard beyond their village. By the time WWI broke out, Finland had experienced an interesting type of autonomy within the Russian Empire. Various governors and the last tsar, Nicholas II, attempted to slowly change Finnish society from the top down through Russification. But between an incompetent, indecisive tsar and an emergency within and outside Russia, Finland was left relatively unmolested in the years leading up to and during WWI.

Throughout that time, the Finns, the Finnish Parliament, and the Senate (which played the role of Cabinet and a sort of Supreme Court) had been gaining more and more power. By the time Lenin signed the independence document, Finland had, to a large extent, been governing itself for a number of years.

Unfortunately for Finland, the economic gap between those at the top and those at the bottom only increased in 1918. That year, a large segment of the Finnish population still worked in agriculture. The life of a Finnish farmer was incredibly hard, and famine was a recurring feature of Finnish life, especially for those who worked the land. Finland, as you can likely imagine, has a very short growing season, and the soil is quite poor, especially in relation to its neighbors to the south and Sweden, which enjoys the benefit of a slightly warmer climate brought in by warmer currents from the Atlantic. Finland does not have this benefit. Honestly, anyone who worked outdoors in Finland had a tough life in the 19th century. Many Finns migrated to other countries, especially the United States, where the winters were milder. In 1918, Finland was not much different from other countries in Europe and North America. More people were leaving farming, fishing, and forestry for the cities and the promise of a better-paying, steady job at the factories that were being built seemingly every month in southern Finland and its coastlines. However, the country was and still is primarily rural.

The Finns had experienced civil upheaval before, especially during and after WWI, as other nations in Europe did. These were mostly worker strikes and occasional protests by farmers. Both of these groups, but primarily the workers in the cities, had been heavily influenced by the rising tide of European social democracy and communism.

Adding to the usual workers' woes (inadequate housing, medical care, job security, worker safety, and pay) was the fact that many of the working class were seeing that life in Finland had been governed by the upper classes, whether they came from Sweden, Russia, or even Finland itself. While the elite of the country discussed the type of government Finland should enjoy after Russian rule, many of those at the bottom saw nothing but a continuation of rule by the elite. The fact the rulers were Finns made no difference.

For hundreds of years, the farmers and rural workers (miners, tar-pit workers, fishermen, etc.) went through their lives following the dictates of others; at least, that was how it seemed to the most radical and militant of them. The upheaval of the war, the vacuum left by Russian rule, and the fact that the elite seemed determined to "make the rules" without input from the workers almost begged for a revolution. And the fact that there was no official Finnish army or national police meant that it was the right time for a revolution.

Finnish Civil War

The Finnish Civil War began on January 27th, 1918, when armed communist groups (which had been getting arms and support from the Soviets) took control of Helsinki in much the same way the Bolsheviks had seized St. Petersburg in 1917.

When that happened, conservative militia groups, some of which had formed before Finland's independence, and many Finnish officers of the tsar's army fled the city and moved to the western parts of the country. There, they disarmed the remains of the Russian army, which had not been able or unwilling to return home after the Bolsheviks took power. The anti-communist Finns were soon joined by many of their battle-hardened countrymen who had fought with Germany. The anti-communist forces, known as the "Whites," were also reinforced by sizable contingents of German troops and officers, who were sent to Finland by their government to prevent the communist takeover of yet another northern country. The Kaiser and conservative forces in Germany, who were still fully engaged against the Allies in WWI, sent large amounts of weapons and ammunition to Finland to support the Whites against the "Reds" (the communists).

Members of the Female Red Guard of Turku, 1918.
https://commons.wikimedia.org/w/index.php?curid=52071524

When the Finnish Civil War began, the Reds controlled most of the southern part of the country, including the major cities. The Finnish Red Army has been estimated to have had around 100,000 men and women in its ranks when the conflict began, with somewhere near 80,000 in arms, 2,000 of them being women. Unfortunately for the Reds, most of these men and women had no combat experience, and only a few officers did. A number of Russian officers were embedded with the Finnish Reds, but they were too few and not well liked.

The White Army had about the same number of soldiers (who were all male), and like the Reds, most did not have army experience of any kind. However, the returning veterans from the Jägers and many of the Finnish officers from the tsar's army gave the Whites a distinct advantage.

During January and February, the Whites solidified their hold on the northern and central parts of the country and trained their troops as much as possible before they went on the offensive. In April, they were joined by thirteen thousand German troops, which quickly established bases around the Gulf of Finland, forcing the Reds to pay attention not only to the Whites in the north but also to their German allies in the south.

The Finnish Civil War was short. By the middle of May, it was over. A slew of smaller battles had taken place during the winter, but the White Army's seizure of Helsinki (carried out in large part by German troops) and the battles for the cities of Vyborg (Viipuri) and Tampere were the major battles of this short conflict.

However, like most civil wars of any size, the Finnish Civil War was exceedingly violent, and the casualty rate was much higher than one would think for a war that lasted just a couple of months. About twenty thousand Red soldiers died in the war. A much smaller number of Whites, Germans, and some Swedish volunteers perished, numbering about five thousand.

The war was bloody for such a small country, and for the losing Reds, capture often meant death. It's estimated that close to ten thousand Red soldiers and sympathizers were gunned down in what would today be considered a war crime. There was also quite a large number (approximately twelve thousand) of Red prisoners who died in captivity or from hunger, cold, and disease. Nearly one thousand Russians who were sent to help the Finnish Revolution were killed in action. Over 1,500 were executed upon capture. These non-combat killings were not one-sided, as it's believed some two thousand White soldiers were executed by the Reds during the short conflict.

Chapter 10 – Mannerheim and between the Wars

After the civil war, the Whites were in a weaker position than they had been before the war. This was because of Germany. It wasn't as if the Kaiser sent his troops to Finland for nothing. Yes, the Germans were worried about the spread of communism, but altruism was not Germany's sole motivation. With a considerable number of German troops still in the country, the German government leaned on the Finnish Senate (which had been building a new Finnish system even before WWI) and forced a German prince on them to serve as the new king of Finland.

The Senate had no choice but to agree, and German Prince Friedrich Karl (Frederick Charles), who just happened to be the brother-in-law of Kaiser Wilhelm II, was "elected" king of Finland. As a result of this, Marshal Carl Gustaf Emil Mannerheim, who had led the White forces during the Finnish Civil War, resigned from his post.

Mannerheim was a hero to many Whites and much of the Finnish population, despite the calls of many on the left in other countries (both Red Finns in exile in the USSR and left-leaning European parties) that he be tried for war crimes.

When Mannerheim resigned from his position, many Finns wondered if another period of instability was about to begin. The short but violent and wide-ranging civil war meant the Finnish economy had declined rapidly. Hunger affected most of the country, and starvation was the norm in the southern part of the nation. International aid from the United States and western Europe helped to prevent the rise of a worse situation.

The division between Finns over the new German king ended in November 1918 when the Germans laid down their arms. The king, his German advisers, and their troops returned home to their defeated country that December.

Given the nature of the Finnish Civil War and communist propaganda, the Finnish government that came out of the conflict and the very short "German period" was amazingly democratic. On July 17th, 1919, the Constitution Act was passed, creating the first independent Finnish government. The act was amended four times throughout the 1920s, each time clarifying certain laws and the responsibility of governmental bodies.

The new government reflected a compromise of sorts. The more influential Whites wanted an appointed president who had a good deal of authority. The more moderate and popular Social Democrats wanted a more powerful Parliament. In the end, the president retained a great deal of power, but this was balanced by the universally elected Parliament. What's more, the Whites' candidate for president, Mannerheim, lost the election, which was won by the Social Democrats, who aligned with the agrarian Centre Party, which mostly represented the farmers and the rural areas of the country, to form a majority.

Though the presidency was won by a member of the Centre Party, who served from 1925 to 1931, the Social Democrats kept a majority within the country. When the party did not lean to the left as far as some radical members wanted, they split from the party and formed a new one, which advocated communism. In 1922, they won nearly thirty seats in Parliament, but by the end of the decade, most of them had been arrested or deported for revolutionary intent. Finland's new rulers were not going to tolerate Russian-supported communism.

In response to Social Democratic control and what they saw as the rise of communism in Parliament and the rest of Europe, right-wing militants formed a new party in 1929. It was called the Lapua Movement, named after the town in which it was founded.

The Lapua Movement was influenced by the rise of fascist power in Europe. In 1929, there was only one fascist government in Europe, that of Mussolini in Italy, but by 1929 (the year the Great Depression began), Adolf Hitler was one of the leading politicians in Germany. In other countries, such as Poland, for example, fascist and ultra-nationalist ideas began to take hold.

The Lapua Movement had sizable support among the conservative upper classes, but as the 1930s progressed and they and other Finns saw the result of fascist violence in other countries, support for the Lapua Movement, which advocated the use of mass violence against anyone they believed to be on the left, began to wane.

In 1932, a Social Democratic meeting in the southern town of Mäntsälä was violently interrupted by a sizable contingent of Lapua supporters led by General Kurt Wallenius, a former chief of staff of the Finnish army. Within a short time, this disruption escalated into a planned coup d'état, with Wallenius calling on the army and the former Whites to join him in marching on the capital. Luckily for Finland, no one responded to his call to arms, and a speech by President Pehr Evind Svinhufvud convinced the Lapua in Mäntsälä and elsewhere to give up any ideas of trying to seize power. Some eight months later, the Lapua Movement was banned by the government, ironically under the same law they had pushed to outlaw the Communist Party.

Mannerheim (1867–1952)

Writing a short book that spans the whole of Finnish history is hard, to say the least. Making the project even more difficult is the figure of Mannerheim, who was named the greatest Finn of all time in a national poll in 2004. So, please keep in mind that what you are about to learn is really more of a sketch of an amazingly interesting and influential life.

Mannerheim, who is often known more by his preferred title Marshal Mannerheim than his full name (Carl Gustaf Emil Mannerheim), was born into an aristocratic family that originated in Germany. His ancestors moved to Sweden in 1693 and were part of a large German minority that played an important role in trade in many Swedish cities. In the 1700s, the Mannerheims moved to Finland, looking for land and opportunity in the sparsely populated Swedish territory.

When Finland was ceded to Russia in 1809, Mannerheim's paternal great-grandfather, Count Carl Erik Mannerheim, held the most powerful position in the semi-autonomous Russian Grand Duchy of Finland. Mannerheim's grandfather and father were interested in a number of different fields, including industry, and the family made a better than modest income.

Mannerheim during the Winter War, 1939–1940.
https://commons.wikimedia.org/w/index.php?curid=14157305

Mannerheim's mother was Swedish-Finnish and the daughter of one of the richest men in Finland. Combined with Mannerheim's aristocratic title, wealth, and physical presence (he was six feet, four inches tall, and handsome), his own intelligence and amazing story put him in a position to be an influential man in Finland when his country needed him the most.

In 1882, Mannerheim attended a Finnish military academy for the upper class but went missing in his senior year, which resulted in his dismissal. Actually, everyone knew where he was: pursuing his love interest. Despite this, he attended the elite Nicholas Cavalry College in St. Petersburg until 1889, and in 1891, he was in the elite Chevalier Guard Regiment in the Russian capital. After having two daughters, his first marriage to a Russian-Serbian noblewoman ended in a separation in 1902 (they were divorced in 1919).

Mannerheim at the coronation of Nicholas II in St. Petersburg, 1896.
https://commons.wikimedia.org/w/index.php?curid=8686448

Mannerheim's first combat experience came during the Russo-Japanese War. Though the war was a humiliating defeat for the Russians, Mannerheim was awarded for bravery and quickly rose in the ranks. By the time the war ended, he was a lieutenant general.

When the war ended, Mannerheim was sent on a journey through Central Asia to Beijing, with the ultimate goal of finding out if a Russian invasion of sparsely populated western China was feasible to offset British interests in the area. Mannerheim's journey took him all the way to China with a small four-man caravan. They judged the support of Central Asian tribes for China and got an up-close look at the terrain. He arrived in Beijing two years after his journey had begun. One of his stops included a meeting with the thirteenth Dalai Lama of Tibet; Mannerheim was the third known European to meet the Dalai Lama.

When Mannerheim returned to St. Petersburg three years later, he was one of the foremost European experts on China and provided an amazing amount of information on China's economy, modernization, politics, military, influence of Japan, and much else. His trip also began a life-long love of Chinese art, and he managed to learn enough of the language to hold conversations.

WWI

As a Russian army officer during WWI, Mannerheim was the commander of the elite Guards Cavalry Brigade and fought in southwest Russia and Ukraine against the Austro-Hungarians and Romanians. He was again awarded for bravery and was made commander of the 12th Cavalry Division in 1915.

Mannerheim was on leave in St. Petersburg when the Russian Revolution against the tsar succeeded. (This was the February Revolution that put Alexander Kerensky in power. Kerensky and his government were overthrown in the Bolsheviks' October Revolution a few months later.) Mannerheim returned to the front but was relieved of his command shortly thereafter, for he was believed to be against the revolution. He resigned from his commission and returned to Finland to what he believed would be his retirement.

We discussed the Finnish Civil War previously. Mannerheim was the commander of the White forces during the conflict. His role in the atrocities that took place is debated in Finland to this day, but most believe that, at the very least, he had some knowledge of them. Within Finland after the war and to some on the left in the country to this day, Mannerheim was the "White General" and bore the responsibility for many massacres during the conflict.

When the Finnish Civil War ended, there were some in Finland who wished to make Mannerheim the king, but that held no interest for him (nor most Finns). So, he retired once again and visited relatives in Sweden. While there, the influential Mannerheim held talks with the British and Americans. He explained to them his and many of his fellow Finns' opposition to the new German king and Finland's desire to become an independent nation. In October 1918, with Germany's defeat inevitable, Mannerheim was sent to Britain and France to confer with the Allies and seek their recognition of an independent Finland. In January 1918, the Germans, Swedes, French, Norwegians, and Danes recognized Finland's independence. Britain and the United States followed shortly thereafter.

When Friedrich Karl returned to Germany, Mannerheim was elected regent by the Finnish Senate and acted as a uniting executive of the country, though his powers were limited. Most of the time, he just added his signature to new legislation as a formality. The position of regent was discarded after the first presidential election in October 1919, which Mannerheim lost by more than two to one. He then retired to private life once again. His past support of imperial Russia and his membership in the Finno-Swedish aristocracy worked against him.

(As part of his effort to seem more Finnish, Mannerheim took to signing documents with the Finnish version of his first name, Gustaf, "Kustaa." He also simply signed as Mannerheim. He never used Carl. His friends and family called him Gustaf. He hated the name Emil and never used it.)

In 1931, with fascism on the rise in Europe and Stalin firmly and menacingly in charge in the Soviet Union, Mannerheim came out of retirement once again to head the National Defense Council. Though Finland had declared a policy of neutrality after its independence, everyone in the country knew its biggest threat came from the east.

From 1931 until just before the outbreak of the Winter War in 1939, the Finns established, built, and reinforced what became known as the Mannerheim Line. Most of the fortifications on this defensive line were built between the wars. It was located on the Karelian Isthmus south of the city of Viipuri but stretched all the way from the Soviet border to the northern end of the isthmus, which led to the Finnish interior.

Finnish-Soviet relations

The next chapter talks about the famous Winter War, which was fought between Finland and the Soviet Union, but before we can discuss that important event, it's important to understand aspects of the relations between the two countries in the years before the war began.

The Karelian people live in the border area of Finland and Russia. With some exceptions, the Karelians of Finland share much of the same culture as other Finns, though they often speak a particular dialect that sets them apart. The same holds true in Russia. Most Karelians on both sides of the border, if they are members of any church at all, are Eastern Orthodox, while most Finns are Lutheran or non-practicing. Changing times and borders have led families in both countries and segments of the population to occasionally call for the unification of all Karelians in one country. Immediately after WWI and into the early 1920s, before the rule of Stalin made the nature of Soviet communism quite clear, many Finnish Karelians and others pushed for a "Greater Finland," which included much of Russian Karelia. Not knowing what was to come, a considerable number of Russian Karelians were indifferent to these calls to join their Finnish brethren. The brutal nature of the climate and the vast forests meant that, for centuries, most Karelians crossed back and forth across the border at will.

However, the rise of communism and the virulent anti-communism of the Finnish Whites during and immediately after the Finnish Civil War meant that from 1918 to 1922, there was a conflict between White militias and the small but still sizable Red Army in Karelia. Though the Finnish government disavowed the incursions by these militias, Mannerheim, at least for a time, supported them.

In 1920, the Treaty of Tartu between the USSR and Finland recognized the rights of the Karelian people in the USSR to autonomy, and the Finns gained the White Sea port of Petsamo. The treaty also formally annulled the 1809 Treaty of Fredrikshamn, which gave Finland to Russia.

However, by 1922, many Karelians in the USSR, like so many others, were beginning to recognize the nature of the Soviet regime. Soviet Karelian militias formed and voted for secession from the Soviet Union. They were joined by a number of Finnish volunteers, but the Finnish government and army remained out of the conflict, although they secretly sent arms to the rebels.

By the end of 1921 and the beginning of 1922, the Soviets had won their civil war and had begun to establish an iron grip on the country. Exaggerated reports of Finnish support for the Soviet Karelian militias provoked the Soviet leadership, especially the chief of the Red Army, the famous Leon Trotsky, who would later lose a power struggle with Stalin and be assassinated in 1940. Trotsky vowed to "march into Helsinki." The Karelians had no chance, and the "invasion" was crushed by the end of January. Tens of thousands of Karelians fled to Finland. Many communist Finns who had fled after the civil war settled in Soviet Karelia, which they used as a base to recruit disaffected Finns (there weren't many) and to spy on their homeland for the Soviets.

The increasingly inhumane nature of the Soviet regime, the quashing of the Karelian rebellion, Trotsky's call for a "march to Helsinki," Stalin's increasing calls for a restoration of the Russian Empire under communism, Soviet meddling in Finnish affairs, and a huge Soviet military build-up were all factors in the Finns building the Mannerheim Line between 1931 and 1939, despite public Soviet declarations of peace between the two countries.

The Mannerheim Line, 1939.

Chapter 11 – Talvisota/Jatkosota (Winter War/Continuation War)

Finnish troops during the Winter War.
https://commons.wikimedia.org/w/index.php?curid=549346

Before we begin, we want to let you know about another great book from Captivating History called *The Winter War*, whose sole focus is on the Winter War. You can also find that book in a larger collection called *The Eastern Front*, which covers the entire war between Germany and the Soviet Union from 1941 to 1945. This chapter will be a relatively short overview of the war between Finland and the USSR in the winter of 1939/40.

In 1932, the USSR signed a non-aggression pact with Finland, Poland, and the Baltic nations of Latvia, Lithuania, and Estonia (all formerly part of the Russian Empire). This surprising move was born from a desire to create a buffer zone between the USSR and resurgent Germany. It was also meant to reassure the smaller countries that they wouldn't fall into Germany's orbit in the near future.

To a smaller degree, the Soviets wanted to ensure, as much as possible, a neutral western flank in the face of a powerful Japan, which had recently invaded the Chinese territory of Manchuria, which lay on the Soviet border.

Though Stalin was firmly entrenched in power in Moscow, the true face of Soviet communism was slowly being revealed to those in the West. None of the nations that signed the non-aggression pact trusted the Soviets, although that was almost always the case when countries sign such pacts. Nations act in their self-interest; trust is another matter.

However, by the late 1930s, Stalin's purges of his real and imagined political rivals and the show trials and executions that followed showed the nations on the borders of the USSR Stalin's true face. Between 1937 and 1938, Stalin purged the leadership of the Red Army, assuring his place at the top but weakening the army to a dangerous degree. But for the Finns, Stalin's military purge was a gift, for the men who led the coming invasion of Finland were not the Red Army's best. Many of them were either killed on the battlefield or in Stalin's prisons afterward.

Throughout the 1930s, the Soviet Union and Hitler's Germany played a game of cat and mouse for influence and control over the Baltic nations, Poland, and Finland. The Finns were, as you know, between a rock and a hard place geographically. To the west lay Sweden, which was an officially neutral and second-class power. In the very north of the country, Finland and Norway shared a small border, which was both out of the way and militarily useless. The only other nation Finland shared a border with was the Soviet Union, and having already fought Soviet-supported communists and the Bolsheviks in Karelia, the Finns were extremely wary of their giant neighbor.

The Finns exported natural resources to the Soviets and received both cash and grain in return. Aside from Sweden (from which the Finns bought high-quality weapons), Finland's other major trading partner was Germany. The Germans needed Finnish minerals and wood, and the Finns needed German machines, machine parts, and arms. The Finns enjoyed a relatively cordial relationship with the Germans before WWI, as well as during and after the conflict.

For the Finns, friendly relations with Germany were the best way to hedge Russian aggression, especially after the rabidly anti-communist Hitler took power. For Hitler, good relations with Finland made Stalin think that he might have a possible northern front to deal with should there ever be a war with Germany, which he expected to happen.

In the last half of the 1930s, the Finns reached out to Estonia, Latvia, Lithuania, and Sweden in an attempt to forge a kind of military alliance on the Baltic Sea, but the nature of the geography (most of the countries were separated by water, with small or non-existent navies) and the relative sizes of these nations, compared to the military giants of the USSR and Germany, caused this effort to fail.

Though Finland's relationship with Hitler was good in the late summer of 1939, Hitler was Hitler. The infamous Nazi-Soviet non-aggression pact, officially known as the Molotov-Ribbentrop Pact (the foreign ministers of the USSR and Germany, respectively) saw Hitler and Stalin agree not to go to war with one another. They also secretly parceled out northeastern Europe between them. In return for Hitler's valuable half of Poland, he agreed that Stalin could take the eastern part of Poland, the Baltic states, and Finland. This would allow Stalin to reconstitute the former Russian Empire, albeit under the red flag of communism. Neither power expected the non-aggression pact to last very long, but Stalin surprisingly expected it to last much longer than it did (it lasted just under two years).

On September 1st, 1939, Hitler invaded Poland from the west. On September 17th, Stalin's forces invaded from the east. They also quickly took over the small and militarily weak Baltic states. In all four countries, the Red Army and Stalin's secret police began a purge of known anti-communists, the intelligentsia (professors, teachers, writers, artists, etc.), and the military, although other groups were persecuted as well. Suspicion of being anti-Soviet was enough to get one thrown in prison. Many didn't even make it to prison.

As the Germans began mass killings of the Jews in Poland (among many other minority groups), tens of thousands of Poles, Latvians, Lithuanians, and Estonians suffered the same fate. When the Germans marched eastward in 1941, many of the Baltic people joined them in an extremely violent anti-communist purge, which had vicious elements of anti-Semitism.

Many Finns saw the writing on the wall; they would be next. First, though, Stalin made demands. On and off during the 1930s, the Soviets had offered to buy or lease a number of Finnish islands off the southern coast of the country. The Soviets wanted these as naval and air bases to protect approaches to St. Petersburg. After Finland won its independence, it was not in the mood to part with any of its territory. When the USSR's offers were rebuffed, veiled and not-so-veiled threats of Soviet military action were made. The Finns rebuffed these as well and continued fortifying the Mannerheim Line and other points along their border and coast.

Shortly after completing his takeover of the Baltic states in October, Stalin made another offer to the Finns: give up the islands in the Gulf of Finland, allow a Soviet base near Helsinki, and give up the Karelian Isthmus. The Finns were determined to protect their hard-won independence and knew that any toehold the Soviets received in Finland would likely end it. So, the Finns sent Stalin "a hard no." By this time, Mannerheim was again in command of all Finnish forces.

During the last part of October and through November, the Red Army built up its strength on the Finnish border. This was done relatively openly, as Stalin hoped the show of massive strength would cause the Finns to cave to his demands. It had the opposite effect.

(It should not surprise anyone that the Finns and Ukrainians have very close relations now and that the Finns have sent a large amount of military and economic aid to Ukraine in its fight with Russia.)

"Forts, cannons and foreign aid will not help unless every man himself knows that he is the guard of his country." Mannerheim

On November 26th, 1939, Soviet secret police agents shelled their own post on the Finnish border in a false flag operation that was blamed on the Finns. No one in their right mind believed the Finns would launch a preemptive attack against their gigantic and powerful neighbor.

On November 30th, 1939, the USSR invaded Finland. It also sent its bombers to Helsinki, causing minimal damage but outraging much of the world. In response, Soviet Foreign Minister Vyacheslav Molotov announced the Soviets had not bombed Helsinki but actually dropped food packages. The Finns called these "Molotov's bread baskets." When Finnish troops engaged the Soviets shortly thereafter, one of their primary weapons against the lightly armored Soviet tanks in the dense and dark forests of Finland were bottles of flaming liquid (with gelatin and naphtha included to stick it to the desired target). The Finns quickly dubbed them "Molotov cocktails."

Soviet attacks from late November to late December 1939.

Most people believed the Finns would either be defeated easily or come to terms quickly with Stalin. Neither happened. All along the Mannerheim Line, the Finns held strong in the face of incredibly careless Soviet assaults, mowing down thousands of Soviet soldiers in days.

Though most of the fighting of the Winter War took place on the Mannerheim Line and was relatively static, the most famous image of the war was the Finnish ski troops in the forests to the north of the Karelian Isthmus. Most Finns then and to this day know how to cross-country ski. Many were experts at it. Covered in white camouflage, virtually silent on their skis, and knowing the country like the back of their hands, the Finns north of the isthmus fell back from the front lines in good order under massive Soviet attacks and lured the Red Army into the depths of the Finnish forests. There, mostly at night but many times throughout the day too, the Finns appeared behind Soviet lines to the left and to the right—they seemed to come out of nowhere. Many Soviet soldiers were killed or wounded by friendly fire because they simply did not know where the Finns were and panicked.

Finnish troops along the front in the trenches of the Mannerheim Line and in the forests to the north showed incredible bravery. This was doubly so when it came to the hundreds of Soviet tanks that took part in the invasion. For the first part of the attack, the Soviets launched tank attacks without supporting infantry. The Finnish soldiers, whose outfits allowed them to blend in the snow and forest, would get close enough to the Soviet tanks that they could place specially made anti-tank grenades in the exhausts or vulnerable spots in their armor. Molotov cocktails in air vents roasted Soviet crews alive.

Three of the Finns' biggest victories were along the Mannerheim Line and at Tolvajärvi and Suomussalmi to the north. In the north, the Finns lured the Russians deep into a forested area that was laced with large lakes. There were only limited areas where troops could travel between the lakes, and the Finns skillfully herded tens of thousands of Russian troops deeper and deeper into the forest. Within days, thousands of Soviet soldiers were killed. Others froze to death. Thousands simply gave up. Only one hundred Finnish died.

In January, Stalin called a halt to most offensive operations in Finland. To say he was displeased would be an understatement. He appointed a new general, Semyon Timoshenko (a future Soviet hero of WWII), to command the effort against Finland and gave him much freer rein than he had with the previous commander. It did not pay to be too much of a free-thinker in the Red Army, but Timoshenko ordered new training, tactics, and clothing and gathered new supplies for an offensive that began on February 11th, 1940.

Simo Häyhä, the greatest sniper of all time and a Finnish national hero.
https://commons.wikimedia.org/w/index.php?curid=18849139

The Finns fought valiantly. You may know of one of the most famous soldiers of the war, Simo Häyhä, the greatest sniper in history. However, the Finns were outnumbered by almost ten to one by the time the Soviets launched nearly half a million men up the Karelian Isthmus. Using new tactics and combined air, tank, artillery, and infantry attacks, the Soviets forced the Finns farther and farther back into mainland Finland.

By mid-February, Mannerheim and the Finnish government knew that it was only a matter of time before the Soviets achieved a major breakthrough and sent word to the Soviets of their willingness to negotiate. The Finns knew they were in a weak position and hoped that the Soviet demands would not be excessive.

At the end of February, Stalin was fearful that a longer war in Finland might cost him more casualties than he was willing to accept in the face of a growing threat from Hitler. So, Stalin dictated terms that were more than the Finns wanted to give up but less than they had feared Stalin would offer. At the beginning of March, the Soviets launched a massive offensive that pushed the Finns almost completely off the Karelian Isthmus and inflicted massive casualties on the tired and now ill-equipped Finnish forces. Attacks farther to the north allowed the Soviets to advance there as well.

On March 12th, the Finns signed an agreement with the Soviets. The agreement did the following:

- Finland gave the entire Karelian Peninsula and a considerable area beyond it to the USSR. Much of southern Finnish Karelia was made Soviet territory.

- In the far north, a large area around the town of Salla was given to the Soviets.

- A number of Finnish islands in the Gulf of Finland were given to the Soviet Union.

- And the island fortress of Hanko on the southwestern coast of Finland was also ceded to Stalin.

Though these concessions were distasteful in the extreme to the Finns, they knew they had no choice. Mannerheim and his officers had fought a brilliant campaign, but the numbers were not on their side, and no ally was going to come to their aid. Understandably, no Finn, then or now, likes to hear this, but considering the possible alternative, the concessions made in 1940 to the Soviet Union were amazingly light.

Part of the reason for that "lightness" was Stalin's fear of Hitler, but most of it was due to the massive casualties the Finns had inflicted on the invaders. Stalin realized what the price would be if he fought a long war in Finland.

Jatkosota

Stalin's attack on Finland drove the Finns further into Germany's orbit. There were thirteen months between the end of the Winter War (March 1940) and Hitler's invasion of the USSR (June 1941). During every month, from March to June, Finland and Germany became closer. The number of German weapons (mostly in the form of small arms and anti-tank weapons) that flowed into Finland skyrocketed, and Finland's trade with Germany also increased.

Politically, there was no question of Finland adopting Nazi policies, unlike other countries closer to Germany. Throughout WWII, the Nazis pressured the Finns to pass anti-Semitic legislation in their country. At times, the Nazis offered to take the Jews of Finland "off its hands," so to speak, but Germany's suggestions were either ignored or openly rebuffed. The Finns had just fought against one totalitarian dictator; they had no desire to slowly give up their independence to another.

When Hitler notified Mannerheim that Germany would be going to war with the Soviet Union and that he considered any of the recently lost Finnish territories to belong to Finland, the two countries came to an understanding. Hitler would gain Finland's support in the north, hopefully causing the Red Army to move troops from their border with Germany in Poland. German troops could be stationed on Finnish soil.

In return, the Finns would reclaim their recently lost territories, which would be recognized by Germany as Finnish. However, Mannerheim and the Finnish government made it very clear that Finland's goals would include nothing but the recovery of lost territory and that Finnish troops would not advance past the borders. Hitler agreed, and oddly enough, even when it became apparent to anyone (other than Hitler) that the war was going badly for Germany, the German leader never caused trouble within Finland, such as, for instance, attempting to place a pro-Nazi Finn at the head of the Finnish government.

Shortly after Hitler's invasion of the USSR on June 22nd, 1941, it became apparent that he would not need the Finns to go beyond their borders at all. The German forces were sometimes gaining close to a hundred miles a day or more. Hitler and many German generals prematurely began to believe that the Soviet Union was finished.

In the north, a German division joined the Finns when Finland declared war on Stalin on June 25th, 1941. Within weeks, Finnish soldiers had almost pushed the Soviets back to the pre-Winter War border on the Karelian Peninsula. Farther north, Finnish and German troops pushed the Soviets rearward but not with the speed that occurred farther south. The forests were thick and slowed the Soviet withdrawal and the Finnish/German advance, though by winter, much of the land that had been lost to the Red Army in 1939 and 1940 was regained.

Throughout the war, the Finns did not advance beyond their stated goals. It must be said that about 1,400 Finns volunteered to join the Nazi Waffen-SS, the armed combat branch of the SS. Throughout the first two years of the war, Finnish SS volunteers fought on the Eastern Front, far south of their home country. By 1943, they had lost about 25 percent of their strength, and during their home leave in the summer of 1943, they were dissolved by the Finnish government.

Throughout Hitler's empire, small segments of many nationalities joined volunteer units of the Waffen-SS. In keeping with Nazi ethnic theories, only people deemed "Germanic" were accepted initially, but as more countries fell under Hitler's control and more foreign volunteers were enrolled, things began to change. By the end of the war, distinctly non-Germans, such as Albanians, Frenchmen, Ukrainians, and others, made up about a third or more of the strength of the Waffen-SS, a force that numbered close to a million men in total. The vast majority of Finns were, if anything, anti-Nazi. They were just anti-Soviet and anti-Russian. *Jatkosota* (the "Continuation War") went just as well as you might imagine. Throughout the war, Soviet divisions were sent to the north to keep the Finns from advancing should they change their minds about their war aims. Though rather small in size in comparison to the battles that took place farther to the south, which included hundreds of thousands of men at a time, serious fighting still took place between the Finns and Germans on one side and the Soviets on the other.

But though the Finns held their own along the border, the same could not be said for the Germans in mainland Europe. That story has been told millions of times: the German defeats at Stalingrad and Kursk, the absolutely huge Soviet military, millions of tons of aid from the US and UK to Stalin, and the need for Hitler to defend Africa and western Europe all contributed to the eventual defeat of Hitler.

The Finns were among the first to see the writing on the wall, which became even more clear when Hitler visited Finland for Marshal Mannerheim's seventy-fifth birthday, which was declared a national holiday. One of the more amazing and rather unknown things about WWII happened during Hitler's meeting with Mannerheim in a train car in Finland.

A Finnish radio technician, who was there to record and broadcast any public statements the leaders wished to make, saw that the window of the train cabin where the leaders were to meet was open. Without anyone noticing, he was able to slide a small microphone over the edge of the window and record about eight minutes of Hitler and Mannerheim's private conversation. The recording is the *only* recording of Hitler speaking in his conversational voice, meaning he was not giving a ranting speech or press interview, which were increasingly rare after WWII began. It is also the only recording of Hitler speaking to a foreign head of state.

Hitler was a bit in awe of Mannerheim, which was clear when he spoke about him among his cronies and when they met. (Mannerheim had visited Nazi Germany in 1934.) Mannerheim was considerably taller and better looking than Hitler, and he had been a general since Hitler was in his teens. Mannerheim was also a foreign aristocrat. Hitler had often shown an old-fashioned and middle-class deference to members of the aristocracy.

Mannerheim was formal, but he was almost always formal. He did call Hitler "polite" and "informed" in their meeting, but many in Finland knew that Mannerheim didn't love Hitler. Throughout the conversation, at least the bit that was recorded, Hitler referred to the huge size of the Red Army and said that if he had known how extensively armed Stalin was, he never would have ordered an attack on the USSR. At that moment, Mannerheim realized that Hitler was not as sure of victory as he claimed. (If you are interested in hearing the full conversation, a link to it is in the bibliography.)

In the summer of 1944, in conjunction with the Anglo-American offensive in France, the Soviets launched a massive offensive along their front line with the Germans and the Finns. Operation Bagration included three million Russians. Only a fraction of those three million was involved in Finland, but that was more than enough. There were few German troops left in Finland, and those that were there were relatively demoralized, as were many Finns. For the Finns, the war had become a war of attrition, and though they were not at the end of their strength, they were fast approaching it.

From June 9th to September 18th, 1944, the Soviets attacked in great strength northward up the Karelian Isthmus. Smaller offensives occurred farther north. Though the Finns inflicted heavy losses on the Soviets, it was clear to everyone that it was only a matter of time before the Soviets took the entire country—a fate virtually no one in Finland wanted. A political squabble resulted in Mannerheim becoming president of Finland and commander in chief, and his government agreed to the Soviet Union's terms.

Those terms included, as you can imagine, the return of the Finnish territories that had been taken by the Soviets in the Winter War, reparations, the ceding of the port of Petsamo on the Arctic Sea, an openly stated policy of neutrality, and closer economic ties to the Soviet Union. Finland was in no real position to disagree.

Those Finns living in the areas that were to be given to the Soviets fled as quickly as they could, as did many Germans. Part of the agreement with the Soviets stipulated that the Finns disarm, by force if necessary, all German troops in Finnish territory. Some German troops were disarmed, but they remained in Finnish, not Soviet, custody. Most returned home. Some German units refused to lay down their arms, and battles did occur between the former allies. The Germans fought a fighting retreat and acted as the Germans had throughout the war, burning thousands of homes and other buildings on their way.

During the Winter War and the Continuation War, Finland lost over ninety thousand soldiers killed in action. Over 150,000 were wounded.

Conclusion

At the end of WWII, Finland entered into a completely new phase of history. The terms of the Soviet agreement were harsh, but they could have been much worse. The reparations payments demanded by Stalin caused a great deal of disruption to the war-weakened Finnish economy. The terms of the agreement did not forbid Finnish contact or trade with the West, but trade was limited due to the state of the Finnish economy and worries over angering Stalin.

Marshal Mannerheim passed away in 1952, ending a long era. That same year, Finland began to come out of the shadow of WWII and hosted the Winter Olympics in Helsinki. Finland did not suffer diplomatically to any great extent with the Western powers after the war. While most nations were not pleased that the Finns had aligned with Hitler, they knew the Finns were truly "between a rock and a hard place" when it came to Hitler and Stalin. Most foreigners were well aware that the Finns had refused to advance past the pre-war borders of 1939, and there was no evidence that the Finnish government or any of its branches had taken part in Hitler's crimes against humanity.

During the Winter War, France, Britain, and the US were all on the side of Finland. While Finland's reputation had been damaged to a degree by its dealings with Hitler, by the early 1950s, it was once again welcomed into the community of free nations to a degree.

That "degree" was determined by Finland's giant communist neighbor. The terms of the post-war agreements with the Soviets included:

- The territorial concessions already mentioned;

- A non-aggression pact between the two nations (neither side—
  although it really only meant Finland—could enter into an
  alliance directed against the other. This was firmly aimed at
  Finland joining the Western powers, specifically NATO after
  it was formed in 1949);

- For fifty years, the Finns would lease the naval base at
  Porkkala to the Soviets. This was later moved to another
  location close by, which today is a beautiful national part;

- The Finns would legalize the Finnish Communist Party and
  outlaw far-right/fascist parties, though its democratic
  government was unchanged;

- Reparations in the amount of $300 million (approximately
  $4.5 billion in 2021);

- Finland's armed forces would not be any larger than deemed
  necessary for the defense of its borders;

- The Soviet Union would be "consulted" of any Finnish
  application to economic pacts involving other states,
  especially with the US and western Europe.

Though Soviet restrictions on what Finland was realistically able to
do internationally relaxed after Stalin's death in 1953 and again in
1956 after Khrushchev came to power in the USSR, the Finns were
cautious in their dealings with the West. Even their desire to join the
Nordic Council, which consisted of Sweden, Norway, Iceland, and
Denmark, was viewed with suspicion, as the latter three countries were
members of NATO. Finland did become a member of that council,
and as the decades passed, Finnish trade with the West grew.
However, it was rather small in comparison with the trade the Finns
engaged in with the Soviets, its satellite nations in eastern Europe, and
the non-aligned nations of the world.

Finland was not isolated from the West like other nations, such as
East Germany, Poland, Hungary, and other Soviet client states, but it
was not integrated with the West either. The country was situated in a
strange sort of diplomatic twilight zone between West and East. The
interesting thing about that is the Finns were free to find their own

unique way into the future. They had a policy of neutrality and were independent of the many rules that came with membership in NATO, the European Economic Community, and the European Union. This place between the West and East and Finland's adjustment to it is known as "Finlandization." The term is often used in situations where smaller countries find themselves caught in the struggle between the larger powers of the world.

After all, the Finns had only been independent since 1917; in other words, in 1945, Finland had been independent for only twenty-eight years. Though the Finnish democratic institutions were strong enough to survive the Cold War, Finland's economy suffered a number of times in the years from 1950 to 1995 (when it joined the EU) and beyond.

Finland played a vital role in Cold War international relations. Helsinki became a hub of spy networks, where the West could spy on the Soviet Union more directly, but the Soviets were able to monitor Western activity in Finland and other parts of Europe from there as well. The Finnish government often brokered back-channel agreements between the superpowers, and in 1975, Finland was the host of talks called the Helsinki Conference. The conference not only led to limits on nuclear armaments in the USSR and the US but also laid down in writing the expected behavior of nations in regard to human rights.

Like its Nordic neighbors, Finland established a very wide social safety net in the years after the war. Though that net has been trimmed back in recent years, the Finns, like the Swedes, Norwegians, Danes, and Icelanders, enjoy a kind of social and educational security unheard of in many other Western countries, including the United States.

The story of Finland is much more than the political and territorial history that we have written here. For instance, Finland's prime minister (as of 2022) is a woman, and Sanna Marin was not the first. Achieving gender equality in Finland and other Nordic nations has been a priority. Finland has been recognized as one of the leading nations in the world when it comes to equality between genders. Finland is also at the forefront of the movement toward equality for LGBTQ people.

As of this writing, for the last five years, Finland has been ranked as the "happiest nation on Earth" in that famous yearly poll of international experts. The Finnish enjoy a high standard of living.

Some of the most pressing problems today include immigration and the limits of the Finnish economy and society imposed on it by immigration. Like many other European nations, especially the richer nations of northern Europe, the influx of refugees from the Middle East has caused Finns to debate the limits of its welfare state and the future of its unique culture.

Other issues that regularly appear in the Finnish news are the autonomy and economic and demographic situation of the Sami people, who were known for centuries, quite to their chagrin, as "Lapps" or "Lapplanders." Various groups of Sami inhabit the central and northern areas of Norway, Sweden, Finland, and, to a small degree, the Karelian Peninsula of Russia. The Sami of the Nordic countries enjoy an autonomy that allows them, within certain limits, to govern and police themselves.

You may know of the Sami people through their famous public image of being reindeer herders, but today, most Sami people in Finland and elsewhere do not make their living in herding, much of which is done for tourist purposes today. Questions about the economic future of the Sami, as well as who the Sami are, are big questions in Finland today. In 2022, some leading Sami questioned Prime Minister Marin's commitment to the well-being of the Sami and posed economic and environmental questions that involved them and their ancestral lands. (We have included links for more information on this issue and on the Sami in general in the bibliography.)

The flag of the Sami of the Nordic nations.
https://commons.wikimedia.org/w/index.php?curid=491498

This book ends where it began, with the end of the century-old policy of Finnish neutrality. Before the Russian invasion of Ukraine, most Finns continued to believe that the official policy of neutrality should continue, though most Finns clearly leaned to the West in terms of identification and culture. Vladimir Putin's behavior in the 2010s and onward caused the number of Finns supporting closer ties to the West to grow, although most Finns did not express a desire to join NATO. The Russian invasion of Ukraine in 2022 changed that opinion literally overnight.

For its size, Finland is exceedingly well armed. It is also well prepared and sends a large amount of economic and military aid to Ukraine. As you can imagine, this has not sat well with Putin and many of the Russian people. In late December 2022, a group of masked men threw bricks and sledgehammers at the Finnish Embassy in Russia. Russian police stood idly by, which tells you quite a bit about Russo-Finnish relations. (A link to the video of this event is in the bibliography.)

It is a time of great change for Finland. During the Winter War, the Finns' stoic courage in the face of the Soviet invasion was known as *sisu*, and today, that word is popular once again in Finland. The country has taken a firm stand against Russian aggression, just as it did back in 1939.

Here's another book by Captivating History that you might like

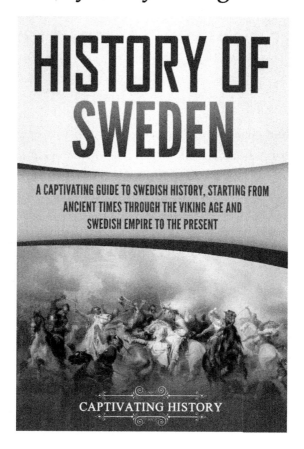

Free Bonus from Captivating History (Available for a Limited time)

Hi History Lovers!

Now you have a chance to join our exclusive history list so you can get your first history ebook for free as well as discounts and a potential to get more history books for free! Simply visit the link below to join.

Captivatinghistory.com/ebook

Also, make sure to follow us on Facebook, Twitter and Youtube by searching for Captivating History.

Bibliography

Anti-Finnish Russian demonstration. Video, December, 20, 2022
https://twitter.com/AlexandruC4/status/1605201446072639488

Accessed October 29, 2022.
https://www.news.com.au/finance/work/leaders/sanna-marin-finnish-pms-photo-shoot-for-trendi-magazine-sparks-social-media-outcry/news-story/f01426d473d991b924775f9f3d3e9d2e

"Dancing Up a Political Storm." The New York Times - Breaking News, US News, World News and Videos. Last modified August 30, 2022. https://www.nytimes.com/2022/08/30/style/sanna-marin-partying-finland.html

Derry, T. K. History of Scandinavia: Norway, Sweden, Denmark, Finland, and Iceland. Minneapolis: University of Minnesota Press, 2000.

"Finland PM Sanna Marin 'Doesn't Care About Rights for Sámi People.'" Euronews. Last modified October 28, 2022. https://www.euronews.com/my-europe/2022/10/27/finland-pm-sanna-marin-doesnt-care-about-human-rights-for-sami-people-as-reforms-likely-to.

"Finland: Monthly Average Temperatures 2021." Statista. Last modified January 6, 2022. https://www.statista.com/statistics/743043/monthly-average-temperatures-in-finland/.

"Finland." Central Intelligence Agency - CIA. Last modified September 7, 2022. https://www.cia.gov/the-world-factbook/countries/finland/.

"The History of Finland." Edrawsoft. Accessed October 29, 2022. https://www.edrawmind.com/article/history-of-finland.html

"The History of the Sami." LAITS – Liberal Arts Instructional Technology Services. Accessed December 19, 2022.

https://www.laits.utexas.edu/sami/dieda/history.htm

"Museovirasto (en-US)." Museovirasto. https://www.museovirasto.fi/en/.

"Mysterious Prehistoric Sites of Finland." SpottingHistory.com - Explore Historic Sites & Historical Attractions on Map. https://www.spottinghistory.com/featured/mysterious-prehistoric-sites-of-finland/

"Salme Ship Burials." Viking Archaeology - Viking Archaeology. https://viking.archeurope.info/index.php?page=salme-ship-burials.

Tacitus. "Germania by Tacitus." Roman History Site and Discussion Forum | UNRV.com. https://www.unrv.com/tacitus/tacitusgermania.php

The Hitler Mannerheim Recordings. (n.d.). YouTube. https://www.youtube.com/watch?v=oET1WaG5sFk&ab_channel=HistoryCh annel "The Transition to Christianity." National Museum of Denmark. https://en.natmus.dk/historical-knowledge/denmark/prehistoric-period-until-1050-ad/the-viking-age/religion-magic-death-and-rituals/the-transition-to-christianity/.

"Vaka Vanha Kalevala Viehättää Yhä Taiteentekijöitä – Taistelu Sammosta on Suosikkiaihe." Yle Uutiset. Accessed December 6, 2022. https://yle.fi/a/3-12683309?s=03.

Varjus, Seppo. "Uutuuskirja: Mannerheim Innostui Aluksi Hitleristä." Ilta-Sanomat. Accessed December 20, 2022. https://www.is.fi/kotimaa/art-2000005187079.html Mannerheim's impressions of Germany, 1934.